Advance Praise for *Being B...*

M000213943

...., __ ___ ...

Eric has created a rock-solid picture of what wealth is and how you accumulate it successfully. Very few people understand the mindset of creating abundance the way Eric has in his life and in this book. If you have any blind spots on money, wealth, or fulfillment in any part of your life, then *Being Broke Sucks, So Stop It* is for you.

—Kris Krohn, Founder of Limitless and Strongbrook

I am putting this book on my shelf with my two all-time favorites *Think and Grow Rich* and *The Science of Getting Rich.*

An excellent book that step-by-step teaches the reader a process of success that can be applied in many areas of life. If you go through the exercises in the success journal, positive changes are inevitable. I felt that Eric was right there with me in person every step of the way. It is a book that I will read again and again to incorporate the strategies for success in my life. I have read hundreds of books, and this one has distilled the essence of the success process clearly and concisely in a very smooth and easy-to-understand way. This book has restored my hope that I can create the life of my dreams.

—Paul H. Taylor, Financial Advisor and Real Estate Investor

Being Broke Sucks, So Stop It! Can an invitation to change your life be any clearer? In this book, Eric gives you a glimpse into his journey from welfare to wealth. He paints no rosy pictures of his past, yet still offers hope and celebration in a future that can be collectively ours.

—Justin Jepsen, Best-selling Author of *In Search of the Wise Men*

Being Broke

SUCKS

SO

STOP IT!

YOUR JOURNEY TO SUCCESS AND THE
LIFE OF YOUR DREAMS BEGINS HERE

ERIC BAILEY

DEDICATION

This book is dedicated to my beautiful wife, Heather, who has made every good thing in my life possible. You are my rock, my source of comfort, my reason for getting out of bed in the morning. I love you more than words can express.

Table of Contents

CHAPTER 1:

MY JOURNEY

The pathway to the top nearly cost me my life. It was a brisk summer evening in August 2011, and my wife and I were meeting with some friends and relatives for a midnight hike to the summit of Mount Timpanogos. Mount Timpanogos is one of the tallest mountains in the state of Utah, with a peak nearly 12,000 feet high and an estimated eight-mile hike to reach the top. Were we nervous? Absolutely not!

We had been planning this trip for several months, and when the day finally arrived, we were as excited as could be. All twenty of us were giving each other high fives and words of encouragement as we carpooled to the trail entrance. The refreshing summer breeze fanned our faces as we began the long ascent up the side of the mountain.

Hour after hour passed, and as the hike became increasingly more difficult, I began to notice an interesting phenomenon. One by one, those who had previously been the most adamant about reaching the top and helping the rest of us to do so began to turn around and head back down. Those who were seemingly in the best of shape, those whom we believed would be the first to arrive at the summit all began to quit, some of them just minutes away from their ultimate goal. How many times have you done this? How many times have you set out to reach a goal but quit midway into it because it was harder than you had imagined?

It takes a special breed of person to have noteworthy success in any field. Why is it that so many people in the United States are overweight and claim to have the desire to lose weight, but fail to do so? Why is it that so many marriages end in divorce? Why do only 1% of people reach what we call the elite class? The answer is simple: those that fail quit when the going gets tough. Thankfully, my wife and I have never wanted to be labeled quitters, so we made a commitment to each other to reach the top of the mountain *no matter what it took.* There are two types of people in the world: those who will be stopped and those who will not. Even though neither of us is an experienced climber, even though I wasn't in the greatest physical shape, even though it was pitch black and neither of us had a flashlight, we were absolutely determined to reach the top.

After seven long hours of exhausting hiking and climbing, we arrived, huffing and puffing, at the summit of Mount Timpanogos. The view was breathtaking! We could see for miles and miles across the beautiful valley of Utah County. The serenity that we felt there was unmatched by any other experience. We spent a good hour just basking in the glory of the accomplishment. We did it! We actually did it!

Any time you reach a new goal, even a small one, celebrate your victory. It doesn't matter how long it takes you to achieve something. The important thing is that the achievement is done. What counts is that you are just a little bit better today than you were yesterday.

After giving each other one last victory hug and high five, we decided it was time to start heading back down the mountain. As we did so, we came across a very narrow strip of trail that we had successfully crossed on our way up. This part of the trail was only about eighteen inches wide, so the only way to safely go across was to turn sideways, lean our entire body weight against the side of the mountain, and slowly inch our way across. Even though it was the middle of summer, the trail at this point was still completely covered in snow, making the path extremely slippery. My wife, who was ahead of me, began to cross just as she had on our way up, when the unthinkable happened. She slipped on the icy snow, lost her footing, and fell off the side of the mountain. Needless to say, it was one of the most terrifying moments of my life. I didn't know how far she would fall or if she would even be alive when I found her. All I knew was that my wife was falling, and I needed to do everything I could to save her.

Thankfully, Heather had learned that if such a thing happened, she needed to spread her arms and her legs as wide as she could to slow down the rate at which she was falling. She was eventually able to slow herself down to the point that she could stop sliding. She just hung there, seemingly in midair, looking up at me as if to plead with me for an answer to what she should do.

I will forever be grateful that there were other people on that trail that day who were familiar with Mount Timpanogos and who called down to assure her that she would be just fine. They instructed her to simply head to the right to eventually find a trail that would take her safely off the mountain. She nodded to show that she had understood, and then looked up at me. I looked back down at her and realized that if we were going to safely make it down, we needed to stay together. Slowly and cautiously, I began to lower myself down to where she was and, together, we started the journey toward the point where we had been promised we would find the path home.

Because the slope of this part of the mountain was steep, it was covered by snow, and I had worn shoes that had zero tread on them, this was, by far, the most difficult part of our journey. Every few feet I would lose my balance and fall just a little closer to the cliff's edge which, if I fell over, would bring certain death. After an hour and a half of sheer frustration and only about a quarter mile of progress, I finally sat down right there in the snow. I crossed my arms and legs, looked up at Heather, and said, "I can't take this anymore! We have been up here for hours. We aren't making any progress at all. I am tired, I am frustrated, I am sore, and it's just no use! You can go on without me and leave me here to die, or you can go get a helicopter to get me off the side of the mountain, because *I am done!*"

How many times have you felt frustrated when your progress went much more slowly than you had anticipated? What did you do? Did you throw up your hands in defeat as I tried to do on Mount Timpanogos? Or did you press forward with faith, knowing that things would all turn out okay in the end? Thankfully, my wife realized what was going on inside me and that it would have only made matters worse if she allowed herself to be negative like me, so she began to tell me jokes and sing happy songs. At first, this only infuriated me even more, because, as I'm sure you can relate, when you're in a horrible mood, the last thing you want to hear is someone telling jokes and being happy! But little by little, my wife encouraged me to keep putting one foot in front of the other and, very slowly, we began to make progress until we found the path that led us safely off the side of the mountain.

One of the most crucial elements of success is always having a mentor—someone who can encourage you and show you how to achieve your goals in much less time. For me, having a mentor made all the difference, both on Mount Timpanogos and in my business.

There were still several difficult moments on our way down. I slipped many times and had to be guided by those who were always miraculously there in the exact moments that I needed to be caught and helped back up. We ran out of food and water and hadn't brought any sunscreen. We were exhausted, starving, parched, and sunburned. But we made it. Thirteen hours after we began our journey, we finally arrived back at the base of the mountain trail.

I understand how difficult the path to success is. It can even be painful at times, but please do not give up. The amazing feeling that we had that day after achieving such an enormous task is one that I will never forget. It is the gratifying feeling of accomplishment.

My pathway to success in other areas of life has been very similar to my experience on Mount Timpanogos. There have been many ups and downs, many moments of victory and many moments of defeat. I have had to pick myself up when I have fallen and endure the humiliating taunts that have lingered in my head when I have failed. Thankfully, there have been many who have gone before me and reached levels of success that I knew I desired. It is largely because of them that I am where I am today. This is why at each of the seminars I teach, I tell the audience that I do not take credit for the principles that I am about to share with them. The principles that I teach during my seminars and that are contained in this book have come from the many mentors and coaches that I have had along the way. By associating with them, I have learned that there are very specific actions that must be taken if one is to truly achieve success and happiness.

By integrating these principles into my life, I have seen miraculous success. In just a few short years, I went from being grossly over-weight, broke, on welfare, and on the verge of marital destruction to being healthy, fit, wealthy, creating a thriving company, enjoying marital bliss, and being the happiest I have ever been. It is now my privilege to assist others to do the same. I don't know what your dream is or what areas of your life you wish could be better, but I do know that investing the time and energy to read this book and then applying the principles found within are the first steps to achieving it.

In order to get the most out of this book, you will want to have a notebook or journal handy, which we will refer to as your success journal. This will be a way of keeping track of your progress and incorporating a hands-on approach to learning. There will be several times when you will be asked to write in this journal. Please do so.

Skipping these steps would be cheating yourself out of a major part of the learning and growing process that I hope you will experience. You deserve to get the most out of this book. I know you can do it! Congratulations for embarking on this incredible journey to success!

CHAPTER 2:

QUESTIONNAIRE

B efore you continue reading, take a moment to fill out the following questionnaire. Number a blank page in your success journal from 1 to 21 so that you can keep track of your answers. These answers will play a major role in you learning what it takes to create the life of your dreams. Be completely honest. There are no right or wrong answers. The purpose of this fun and enlightening exercise is simply to help you see what areas of your life can be improved, starting with your mindset.

1. You have a major decision to make. You:
   A. Do the most logical thing
   B. Do what everyone else does
   C. Do what your friends and family say you should do
   D. Follow your heart and gut instinct

2. You attend a free class in which the presenter offers a higher-level training that you feel would get you to a higher level of success much more quickly. The cost of the training is more than your monthly income. You:
   A. Resent the presenter for charging so much
   B. Say, "I can't afford that," and do nothing
   C. Delay signing up for the training until it better fits into your budget
   D. Figure out a way to sign up for the training immediately

3. You feel greatly impressed to take a major leap of faith in your life. You:
   A. Ignore the impression because it isn't logical
   B. Have to think about it
   C. Decide to do it, then change your mind at the last minute
   D. Trust your heart and do it no matter what

4. Money:
   A. Is the root of all evil
   B. Isn't that important to me
   C. Is a great tool that can be used for good
   D. Give me more of it!!!!!

5. You find out that someone who is extremely successful and whom you really admire will be hosting a free class two hours away from your home. You:
   A. Wait until there is a class a little closer to your home
   B. Do nothing
   C. Don't attend because you can't afford the gas to get to the class
   D. Get there no matter what

6. You make a decision to do something a bit outside the box. Your parents tell you how foolish you are and try to persuade you to take a different course. You:
   A. Follow your parents' advice. They always know best
   B. Begrudgingly do what they advise out of fear of reprimand
   C. Stick to your decision, but inwardly allow fear and doubt to creep in
   D. Know that your gut instinct is always right and stick to your decision regardless of what other people think or say.

7. You commit to help a friend set up for an event she's hosting. Your friend thanks you profusely for being willing to help. At the last minute before you are supposed to leave, your child throws up all over your shirt. You:
A. Call your friend to explain that you won't be able to help after all
B. Don't show up at your friend's event. After all, you need to get your child to the doctor.
C. Do nothing
D. Clean up and still keep your commitment to your friend

8. Your rich uncle who lives in Africa passes away and leaves a check for $10 million that you have to personally pick up. You don't have enough money to fly to Africa. You:
A. Don't go because you can't afford the trip
B. Do nothing. It was probably a scam anyway.
C. Delay going to Africa until you have successfully saved enough money to go
D. Do whatever it takes to come up with the money and get to Africa to pick up that check as soon as possible

9. Debt is:
A. Something to be avoided at all costs
B. All I focus on; my biggest goal is to get out of it
C. Can be good or bad. I avoid it for frivolous things, but don't mind getting an occasional loan to invest in ways that will ultimately make me a high return
D. I use my credit card and buy anything I want

10. Investing in hiring a personal mentor is:
    A. A poor decision; I don't need anyone else's help
    B. I wouldn't mind having a mentor if they didn't charge anything, but I wouldn't pay for anything like that
    C. Something I would have to think about
    D. One of the best investments I could make. No matter the cost, nothing is a better investment than a person who can help me achieve things I desire in life.

11. People with lots of money:
    A. Are all crooks
    B. Are all selfish and haughty
    C. Are going to hell
    D. Probably worked hard to get where they are

12. Public speaking:
    A. Is my biggest fear and something I would never do
    B. Is something I'd do if I had to, but I wouldn't give it my all. I mean, what if I make a mistake!?
    C. Is scary, but I would do it and give it my all if necessary
    D. Is something I love doing

13. My relationship with my Higher Power is:
    A. Not a priority in my life
    B. I don't have a higher power
    C. Could be better
    D. Amazing

14. Your spouse wants you to take them to a fine-dining restaurant for a special occasion.
    A. That's too much money to spend on one meal!
    B. What's a fine-dining restaurant?
    C. I'll go, but begrudgingly
    D. Sounds awesome! Anything for them!

15. When it comes to personal growth,
    A. I'm happy right where I'm at
    B. I only do personal growth exercises if I don't have to go outside my comfort zone
    C. I want to experience growth, but very slowly
    D. I want to move forward as quickly as I possibly can

16. Your spouse wants to invest in a personal development program. You:
    A. Tell them they aren't allowed to spend money on that kind of thing
    B. Tell them you'll have to think about it first
    C. Let them do so, but don't like the idea of them spending money on that kind of thing
    D. Trust your spouse completely and support whatever decision they make

17. The way you deal with stress is by:
    A. Overeating
    B. I don't. I just bottle it up inside me
    C. Exercising
    D. Other (please explain)

18. Your mentor gives you an action step that seems weird. You:
    A. Don't do it
    B. Find your own way of doing it
    C. Do it halfway
    D. Do it, trusting that your mentor has your best interest at heart and knows what he's talking about

19. How many books did you read from cover to cover in the last year?
    A. 0
    B. 1 to 3
    C. 4 to 9
    D. 10+

20. You see someone younger than you having more success than you. You:
    A. Are jealous
    B. Feel sorry for them
    C. Feel genuinely happy for them
    D. Ask them to teach you how they did it

21. If you could have absolutely any three wishes granted right now, what would they be?

Great job getting this done. For now, simply keep your answers safe in your success journal. We will come back to them later.

CHAPTER 3:

BEGINNING YOUR JOURNEY

One of the biggest mistakes that people make is not having a clear vision of the kind of life they desire. They see what their peers and family members have in their lives and believe that such is the norm. They fail to dream big simply because they don't know that there is a possibility of more than they currently have.

What does your ideal life look like? If you could have absolutely anything you desire and nothing could stop you, what would you want to create? This is the first step in your journey to success. Grab your success journal right now and answer the following question: My ideal life looks like . . .

Be as descriptive as possible. Paint a vivid mental picture for yourself of everything that you desire. This could include a fancy house and car, an amazing spouse and family, a beautiful, athletic body, having millions of dollars in the bank, being able to spend as much time as you desire with your loved ones—the sky is the limit! Once you have this done, read it to yourself out loud, then place your hand over your heart and say, "I'm awesome!"

Now that you have the end in mind, it is important to break things down into both short-term and long-term goals. I once heard someone say that a dream remains only a dream until it is written down. That's when it becomes a goal. What would you like to see yourself accomplish in the next week, month, year, five years, and ten years? Take a moment to answer this question in your success journal.

Whenever I bring up the subject of goal setting, many people say things like, "But Eric, why set goals? I'm really happy right where I am. I'm comfortable. Why change anything? Why fix something if it isn't broken?" I gently remind them that the whole point of life is to progress. An old adage says that if you aren't growing, you're dying. If you aren't moving forward, you're moving backward. If you are capable of improving your life and helping many others do the same, why not do so?

"But Eric, I don't need to be rich to make a difference in the world. Smiles are free, after all." I've heard this objection more times than I can count. Yes, you don't have to be insanely successful to help people, but the rich and successful can help in ways that poor people simply cannot. Who has more control over political decisions, the poor or the rich? Who has more influence over the media, the poor or the rich? Who decides what the fashion trends are, the poor or the rich?

I heard of a story of a woman who was diagnosed with an advanced stage of cancer. The only way that she could have any hope of surviving was to undergo years of intense medical treatments. She had a husband and children, so naturally she agreed to get started. You can imagine how costly this would be. Medical care is not inexpensive, and years of intense treatment would easily cost millions and millions of dollars. Not long after she began, her health insurance cut her off, saying that she had reached her lifetime limit of benefits, and they would no longer help pay for her medical treatments. Needless to say, she and her family were devastated. They did not have a lot of money, and what they did have went toward paying off some of the co-payments that she had incurred along the way. With a heavy heart, she realized that she would not be able to continue her medical care and resolved to die.

One day, she checked her mailbox and found a letter with no signature and no return address. She opened it and read that the anonymous writer knew who she was and knew of her situation. As she opened the letter further, a black titanium credit card with her name on it fell out. The letter continued, "There is no credit limit on this card. Please take it and charge all of your medical expenses to it, and they will get paid." I can only imagine the emotion that must have overcome her as she read those words. What gratitude she must have felt for that nameless individual who helped to save her life that day. An individual who couldn't have saved a life if he hadn't been wealthy.

People ask me all the time, "Eric, why do you talk about money all the time? What's your purpose for becoming wealthy and teaching others to do the same?" First and foremost, someone has to do it. There are enough people in the world who use their money for selfish purposes. I want to help raise a team of wealthy individuals and families who will help to do some good in the world.

What is your personal *Why*? Your *Why* will be what drives you every day. Even when you don't know the "how," your *Why* will help you continue to move forward. Get out your success journal and answer the following question: My purpose for becoming wealthy and successful is . . .

Once you have done this, read it to yourself out loud, then place your hand over your heart and say, "I'm awesome!"

At this point you might be thinking, "Eric, this all sounds great, but am I to expect these results to just pop out of thin air? Am I just going to wake up one day and magically have the skills I need to make all my dreams come true if I have a big enough *Why*?" Of course not. It is a process that happens over time and often requires patience.

I had the privilege of serving as a missionary in South America for a couple of years and was required to learn the Spanish language. I had taken a few semesters of Spanish in high school, but nothing could prepare me for becoming fluent in a language in a very short period of time. I was in a state of *unconscious incompetence*, meaning I didn't know what I didn't know. I had never learned an entire new language before and had no idea how difficult it would be.

How many people do you know that are in this phase right now when it comes to becoming successful? They don't know that it's possible to improve their lives, so they don't even try.

I began my missionary service inside what is called the Missionary Training Center, where I spent nine weeks learning the ins and outs of missionary work and trying to suck down as much Spanish vocabulary and grammar as I possibly could. This opened my eyes to the realization that there was more to learn than one ever could within nine short weeks. I reached a level of *conscious incompetence*.

Do you remember going through driver's education? At first, learning how to drive a car may have seemed daunting. You suddenly learned that there is more to driving than just knowing how to press a gas pedal and turn a steering wheel. You realized that there are traffic laws you're required to know before you ever climb into the driver's side of a car for your behind-the-wheel training.

The fact that you chose to read this book is evidence that you are no longer in *unconscious incompetence* and are, at the very least, in a level of *conscious incompetence* when it comes to success. You have, if nothing else, come to the realization that you need help to learn the principles and laws of wealth if you want to become successful.

After my nine weeks in the Missionary Training Center came to an end, I entered the missionary field and was placed with a companion, another missionary assigned to be by my side 24 hours a day, who was a native Peruvian and didn't speak English. I eventually got to the point where I could think of something I wanted to say in English, use the knowledge I had to interpret my thought in my mind, and then say it in Spanish. I had entered a state of *conscious competence*. I could consciously put into practice what I had learned and use it to effectively communicate with the people of Peru.

Once you completed the behind-the-wheel portion of driver's education, you could consciously bring to mind the various traffic laws that you needed to follow and the basic skills you needed to drive from one place to another. It is my hope that, by the time you finish reading this book, you will enter a state of *conscious competence* when it comes to success by taking the tools you learn and consciously applying them to create higher results in your life.

It was finally after many months of complete language immersion in Peru that I reached a level of *unconscious competence*. I no longer had to stop and think about what another person said to be able to understand them or what I needed to say in order to speak. I simply opened my mouth and allowed the words to come freely out in proper Spanish. This came after great amounts of practice, doing what I had learned over and over again until it came naturally.

If you have a current driver's license, you are probably in a state of *unconscious competence* when it comes to driving. Because you have driven countless times before, you no longer have to consciously think about how to drive; you simply do it. It is my goal with all of my personal mentoring students to help them reach a state of *unconscious competence* when it comes to success. They have spent enough time one-on-one with me, learned all that I could teach them, and practiced the principles that I share with them so much that it becomes second nature. They begin to make choices that bring wealth and success without even realizing it.

When it comes to moving up the levels of success, start with smaller goals, then move on to goals that are a little bigger, and then to goals that may have seemed enormous in the beginning. When I first started my healthcare practice, I set a goal to see just two paying clients a week. At the time, when I was fortunate to see one or two a month, two people in a week seemed like a pretty daunting goal. But I eventually achieved it, and then set the goal to see five, and then ten. Eventually, I reached my goal of seeing 100 paying clients in a single week, a task that seemed impossible only twelve months earlier.

"Eric, going through this process seems really scary to me. Is it really worth it?"

This very thought went through my mind as I climbed Mount Timpanogos. The closer I got to the top, the steeper it became. My lungs felt like they would burst as I gasped for breath during the final 100 yards of the trail, but the feeling of victory when I finally reached the summit made everything I had gone through worth it.

You deserve to live the life of your dreams. You deserve to create the life you've always desired. And once you reach your current goals, you get to set new ones, create new dreams, and then turn around and help others reach theirs.

Never be complacent. Again, if you aren't growing, you're dying. Live the life you desire. You so can.

Now that you have your goals written down in your success journal as well as your purpose for achieving them, let's bring you up to speed on some roadblocks you may encounter along this journey and ways to overcome them.

CHAPTER 4:

THE FILTERS

'll never forget the Christmas that I gave my mom a new water filter. I was about nine years old at the time, and I prided myself on giving the absolute best Christmas gifts in the family (or so I thought). I saw a commercial for an amazing water filter and thought that it would be absolutely perfect for her. I remember doing all of my chores and some extra jobs around the house so that I could earn the money that I needed to purchase this incredible gift.

The day arrived to head to the store. I searched through aisle after aisle after aisle until I finally found it: the exact water filter that I had seen on TV sat pristinely upon the shelf, beckoning me to purchase it. And purchase it I did. I took it to the front, plopped it down on the counter, and joyfully presented my thirty dollars (which, to a nine-year-old, is like millions!) to the cashier, who smiled as she handed me the receipt. I came home as quickly as I could and, with help from my dad, wrapped this enormous gift that I would be able to present to my mother on Christmas Day. My heart bubbled with anticipation as the days passed and Christmas got closer and closer. Finally, during our traditional Christmas Eve dinner, I could take the pressure no more, and I insisted that she open her present. I smiled from ear to ear as she carefully unfolded each layer of wrapping paper, finally revealing the new water filter inside.

I remember watching in awe as she filled it with water and saw each tiny water droplet pass through the miniature holes and drip into the bottom of the container, now clean and purified. The first glass of that water blew me away; I had never tasted water so delicious.

It is no secret that life tends to pass us through its own set of filters. Most of us get caught in traps, while a very small percentage actually make it to what we call the elite class. If so few reach those high levels of success, what happens to everyone else? What is stopping so many people from living the life of their dreams?

In my experience as a mentor and throughout my own journey to success, I've found that there are five major filters, or stoppers, keeping people from reaching their peak potential. These filters include fear, inconvenience, money, embarrassment, and judgment.

Fear

In December of 2013, my wife and I took a leap of faith and invested in a four-day class that would teach us how to become better presenters and trainers. I'm one of those crazy people who actually enjoy public speaking and being the center of attention, so when I found out that there was a class that I could attend and learn how to do this properly and actually get paid for it, I decided that my wife and I were going to get there regardless of what it took to do so.

This class ended up being life-changing for my wife and me. We learned skills and techniques that we would implement in our business daily as we interacted with prospective clients and those who were learning for the first time about what we do.

One of the assignments the instructor had us do was to commit to at least two dates in the coming month on which we would put into practice that which we were learning and give public presentations. Being a man of my word, I kept my commitment and held two three-hour classes in January of 2014 called Creating a More Abundant 2014. They were a huge success! Following the exact template that my instructor had given me, I had each attendee following my every word as they took copious notes, stood up to shout declarations, watched motivational videos, and listened to my story of reaching several inspiring goals that I had set. As the class drew to a close, the time neared for me to introduce a new, full-day class that I was developing and offering at the class for a fee. My heart kept pounding as the time for me to present the idea for this class came closer and closer. "What if I offer this class and not one single person signs up? How will I feel if I did all this work and I don't end up with anything to show for it?" Doubts and fears of every sort kept passing through my mind. Could my ego stand the blow if no one registered for my next class? Wouldn't that mean that I wasn't good enough and that no one liked me? The temptation to skip over the details about the upcoming class without even offering it was overwhelming. I was so close to chickening out and giving in to what I call the *fear filter*.

How many times have you experienced similar circumstances? How many times have you felt impressed to do something, talk to someone, or make something happen, but didn't because of fear? Perhaps you feared rejection, loss, or failure. How is this showing up in your life? How is it affecting your results? Take a moment and answer these questions in your success journal.

Thankfully, the words of one of my mentors came to my mind that day: "Keep your commitment! People need the message that you have to offer!" I offered the class, finished my presentation, and then ran and hid in the other room because I was so terrified that no one would sign up that I didn't even want to be in the room to see whether they did or didn't. I shut the door behind me, buried my head in my hands, and prayed that there would be one, just one single person who would value what I did enough to register for my class.

After several minutes, I finally summoned up the courage to peek out the door to see what was going on. To my surprise, I saw a line of people waiting to fill out a registration form. I couldn't believe it! After all was said and done, I asked my wife how we did, and she told me that we had made more money in those three hours than we had in the entire previous month simply by offering this next-level class. I never would have experienced this great accomplishment if I had allowed fear to stop me from keeping my commitment of offering my next-level training to my audience.

When it comes to overcoming fear, it's important to start by understanding where fear comes from and why it shows up in our lives. Fear usually shows up to counter faith. It is the opposite of faith and often comes into play when a person is about to take some sort of leap of faith.

Would you agree that there is an opposing force in the world that wants to keep us from being happy and successful? And that this force will put as much fear and doubt into our minds as possible when something good is about to happen?

There are many definitions of fear. The one that I believe is the most accurate is "the anticipation of pain." We often stop ourselves from moving toward a particular goal because we believe that we will experience pain along the way. The thing about this type of fear, though, is that it only exists in the future. Think about that. If fear is the anticipation of something, it hasn't happened yet. So it doesn't exist in the past or the present, and the future only exists in our minds.

Not too long ago, I took my employees to a seminar where this principle was beautifully illustrated when the trainer had us all do an exercise that I want you to do as well. Ready? Raise your hand tomorrow. Come on, go ahead, raise your hand tomorrow. Why aren't you doing it? It obviously can't be done because tomorrow doesn't exist. There is only today. Think about that for a moment. If fear only exists in the future, and the future doesn't exist, what does that say about fear?

"Oh, but Eric, fear is something I feel. It isn't logical. Telling me something logical, like 'fear doesn't actually exist in the present,' doesn't help me!" It's true that most of the fears that we experience are emotional, not logical. If this is the case, what can we do about it?

I mentioned that fear is the anticipation of pain, and there are three main categories of pain that fear tends to fall into. The first is what we call "loss pain." Many people don't make investments because they fear losing what they put into it. What if they invest time, money, or energy into something, and they don't see an immediate return on their investment? To combat this type of fear, it is important to focus on the gain. If you are considering investing in yourself, for example, rather than focusing on the money that you will put into it, focus on what you hope to get out of it.

The next type of pain that people fear is called "process pain," or the pain of change. How many people do you know who want to release weight and get fit but don't because they think the process of changing their lifestyle and adopting a new diet and exercise plan will be too painful? As the old saying goes, "When the pain of the situation becomes greater than the pain of change, action is taken." Again, focus on what results you want. Ask yourself if going through the change will be worth it. Most of the time the answer will be yes.

Finally, there is what we call "outcome pain." What if the grass isn't really greener on the other side? What if I quit my job and I don't succeed with this new business? What if, what if, what if . . . ? How many people do you know who want to start a business but don't because they fear the outcome won't be what they hoped? The only way to get through this is to focus on the *Why,* or the purpose for doing whatever it is you want to do. If your *Why* is great enough, the *How* takes care of itself.

Let's go back to the emotional aspect of fear. Our emotional side is controlled by a certain part of the brain, and our logic comes from another part of the brain. Sometimes simply switching to the logical side of your brain when you feel fear can make all the difference. When you start to feel fear coming on, try asking yourself, "How much fear do I feel right now on a scale of 1–10?" The act of going into the logical side of your brain could be enough by itself to dispel the emotion of fear.

But what if this simple exercise isn't enough? What if the fear is more logical than emotional? Examples of logical fear could be that you'll follow in the footsteps of a parent and grandparent who both had a certain bad habit, or that you'll inherit a certain condition that all of your family has struggled with. What do you do then? If this is the case, it's important to find the root of the fear, where it is coming from.

Start by writing down or stating your fear out loud. For example: if you fear failure, you would say or write down, "My biggest fear is failure." You would then ask yourself, "The absolutely worst part of failure would be . . .," and answer the question. Let's say that you felt that the worst part of failure would be feeling like you let your family down. You would say, "The absolute worst part about feeling like I let my family down would be . . .," and keep doing this exercise until you run out of things to say. The very last thing you say or write down is the actual fear that you have. Often this will be something small, albeit deeply rooted.

You can then ask yourself if (whatever it is) is actually something to fear. If the answer is no, you've just overcome your logical fear. If the answer is still yes, you may need to implement one of the following tools:

Did you or any of your children ever believe that there was a monster in your closet or under your bed when you were growing up?

Were yours like most parents who just told you that no, there wasn't any monster in your room and, therefore, nothing to be afraid of? If so, did it get rid of your fear? If you're like most people, probably not. This is because fear needs to be validated, and then action needs to be taken. Rather than telling a child there is no monster in the closet, have them do something like grabbing a squirt gun and spraying a few drops of water on the closet door to "melt the monster." Having them take action to solve the problem will dispel the fear much more effectively than just ignoring it. The same principle applies to adults. If fear is stopping you in your tracks, *do* something about it. Take some sort of action. Don't allow fear to paralyze you, as so many people do. You may find that, the more action you take, the less your fear seems to be a factor in your life.

Quite possibly the most powerful tool against fear is laughter. Back in the late 1990s, author J. K. Rowling introduced the world to Harry Potter, a seven-book series that would introduce us to the magical world of witchcraft and wizardry. In the third book of the series, we are presented with a certain creature (a boggart) that would instantly shape-shift and turn into whatever the nearest person feared the most. Harry's teacher instructed him and his classmates that the only way to counter this type of creature was with laughter and a simple spell (*Riddikulus*) that would turn their fear into something humorous. Rowling may never know just how brilliant this theory was.

I can still remember a nightmare I had when I was just six years old. I was observing a sort of eerie cartoon which took place on top of a tall cliff which overlooked the ocean. There were sharp, jagged rocks at the bottom, leading one to believe that anyone who fell off this cliff would fall directly to their death. I will never forget the terror I felt when I watched in horror as the characters kept getting closer to the edge and the feelings of helplessness I had as I dreaded having to watch one of them fall to his doom.

The emotions I experienced during this nightmare stayed with me for years. There were many times that I would lie awake at night, not able to sleep because the images of this nightmare I had experienced years before just wouldn't go away—until I tried the following exercise:

I was tossing and turning in bed one evening as the image of my nightmare flooded my mind, when I decided to try something unusual. As the view of the cliff became clearer and clearer, I imagined that it had a silly, smiling face that would ask people how their day was going whenever they passed by. Turning the once frightening image into something humorous was enough to dispel the emotional charge of my fear, and, pretty soon, I was no longer haunted by this nightmare.

Try the following exercise the next time you feel fear creeping up on you. Grab a piece of paper and draw a depiction of your fear. It doesn't have to be a masterpiece; just make some sort of drawing that represents what your fear looks like in your mind. Then add something to the drawing to make it humorous. One client who did this exercise depicted his fear as a giant, squiggly ball of fuzz. When asked how he could turn it into something funny, he looked at it for a moment and shouted, "Oh my goodness! That looks just like my hair in the morning!" He attached a head and a face to the ball of fuzz and began to laugh hysterically. This laughter eliminated the emotional charge of his fear, and from then on, if he felt this fear begin to creep up on him, he would instantly picture his hair in the morning. Since, of course, his hair would never harm him and wasn't at all scary, this fear quickly disappeared.

If, after completing this exercise, you still need a little something extra to help you overcome your particular fear, just start laughing. Laugh until you make yourself laugh some more. You may be surprised at how laughter can make a difference in your life and in your results.

In any event, you must take significant and immediate action to combat fear. Fear breeds during periods of inactivity. The longer you wait to take action, the more intense your fear will become. It doesn't matter how many times you tell yourself that there is nothing to fear or that your fear isn't actually real, until you take action, no results will come. Get moving and decide that fear will no longer be a filter in your life.

Inconvenience

Take a moment right now and imagine that you have a relative who lives in Africa. After he passes away, you discover that he was extremely rich and left you a check for $10 million, with the stipulation that you had to fly to Africa and personally pick up the check. There is just one problem: you don't have enough money in your bank account to purchase a plane ticket. What do you do? You may recognize this as question 8 in the questionnaire in Chapter 2. I once posed this very question to those on my social media feed, and some of the answers I received in the comments section surprised me. There were some who replied with things like, "Well, if I couldn't afford a plane ticket, then I wouldn't go." Others said things like, "I would set the goal of raising the money so that I could pay cash for a plane ticket and go pick up the check without guilt." Still others cried out, "I would borrow the money and somehow figure out a way to get to Africa as quickly as possible. I would do whatever it took to achieve my goal."

Take a moment right now and make a list in your success journal of all the reasons why you have ever failed. Seriously. Do it right now. Put this book down and list all the reasons why you have ever failed. Did you get it done? Do not proceed until you have.

If your list is like that of most people, it probably includes things like "I didn't have enough money to get started," or "I didn't have the time," or "I didn't have the right schooling." It's fascinating that each time I teach one of my LIFT OFF seminars, I ask the audience this same question and almost always receive answers similar to the three above. The thing about these answers is that they all list resources, external factors, when the real problem can be found within the individual—a lack of resourcefulness. If you ever find yourself in a situation like the above-mentioned case of needing to go to Africa and pick up a check, unsuccessful people will use a lack of resources, in this case money, as an excuse for why they didn't achieve what they said they wanted to achieve. Successful people, on the other hand, use their resourcefulness, such as tenacity, dedication, determination, and perseverance, to come up with the resources they need when they need them. In this case, they could put the cost of the plane ticket on a credit card. They could borrow the money from a bank or a loved one. They could refinance their car or their house. The point is, successful people do *whatever it takes*, and they do it *no matter what.*

I can't tell you how many people have told me that they are *interested* in what I have to say and would love to come to one of my classes to learn more. They then ask me when I will be coming to their home town. When I respond that I currently have no plans to do so, they act disappointed and express that they would come if it was only a little closer to them. A little inconvenience, this time in the form of a little bit of travel, was enough to stop them from doing what it took to receive the training that they need to be successful.

My friend, the pathway to success is almost *never* convenient! If it was convenient, there would be no growth, for growth only takes place when sacrifices are made. I once had to make a 60-hour round-trip journey to get to a training that ultimately helped me achieve the success that I have today. Not including the cost of travel, the seminar itself cost me thousands of dollars. But I got there. I proved to myself that I would do whatever it took, and my results prove it.

I can't tell you how many people have told me that they are "interested" in the things that I teach and do. They tell me how much of a difference it would make to their happiness if their lives were different and express how much they admire people like me for going first and proving that it's possible. I graciously thank them for their kind words and ask what they are going to do to facilitate their progress. Sometimes they will look at me funny and respond that they weren't going to do anything differently and had no plans to come to any of my seminars. When it comes to success, there are two types of people in the world: those that are "interested" and those that are *committed.* Those that are "interested" are the dreamers, the ones who say how much they would like a better life, sometimes even the ones who show up at the seminars but don't actually apply what they have learned. They usually have excuses for why they aren't where they want to be. Those who are *committed,* on the other hand, learn what they need to do to achieve their desired results, and they make it happen *no matter what.*

Right now, make a list in your success journal of all your excuses. You may find that this turns out to be a rather long list, but get it done. Once you've done this, make a solemn commitment to yourself and to others that you will *never* allow these excuses to be a filter in your life again, and then go destroy the list.

Money

Let's go back to December 2013. My wife and I are at the four-day class learning how to be better presenters. On the fourth and final day, the trainer began to tell us about a six-month program that was available to anyone who desired to further their education and become the absolute best presenter possible. I remember listening to the details of the program and thinking, "This is it! This is the training that I've been looking for! I know I can get my family out of the pit that we are in financially if I can just get this training." I stood up to go sign up for the course . . . and then I saw the price. It was $4,900. Remember, we were on welfare at the time. The price of nearly $5,000 was more than five times what I was making in a month, so I started to sit back down. Thankfully, my wife grabbed me by the arm and said, "I don't think so. Get back there and sign up!"

I pointed at the price and violently shook my head. What was my wife thinking? There was no possible way that I could come up with five thousand dollars, let alone justify spending that kind of money when we were on financial assistance. She continued to look at me with those beautiful, loving eyes of hers and simply asked, "Eric, is it right?" What could she possibly mean by that? Signing up for the six-month course didn't make any logical sense. She continued to look at me and asked, "Does it feel right to you?" After a moment to calm my brain enough that I could get in touch with my feelings, I responded, "You know what? I feel peaceful about it." Her response has become a sort of "mantra" to our family ever since then. She looked me right in the eyes and said, "Eric, if it's right, what else matters?"

I went straight to the back table, picked up a registration form, and began to fill it out. I began to hyperventilate and shake because I was so scared that I was making a mistake. Again, Heather walked up to me and asked me, "Eric, is it right?"

"Yes," I replied.

"Then what else matters?"

I maxed out every credit card that I had that day, but I signed up for the training. Realizing that I needed to take major action and apply everything I learned from this program to the best of my ability, I went to absolutely every training that was included in this program and tried to absorb everything I possibly could. Things in my life began to shift dramatically. As I began to improve as a presenter, my health-care practice began to grow. More and more people started registering for classes that I was teaching, and within just four months, our income quintupled. I reached a point where I was making more money each month than I had ever made, which was much, much more than I had invested in the six-month program. I had invested in myself, and I received a return.

The key to overcoming the money filter is to find ways to invest in yourself. Remember that your mind is your greatest asset, and learning just one new skill can make the difference between mediocrity and success. Read books, listen to audio trainings, go to seminars, and hire a good personal mentor. Get as much education as you possibly can, and not just the kind that takes place in classrooms. Develop new skills, and then use them to create a return on your investment.

Robert Kiyosaki, best-selling author of the book *Rich Dad, Poor Dad*, is one of my favorite examples of this principle. It has been said that Robert earns an estimated $2 million per month in passive income, largely from his real estate investments. He explains that he first learned how to do this by investing, years ago, in a $500 seminar which would teach him all about the fundamentals of real estate. As he was signing up for the class, he notified one of his neighbors of the class and asked him if he would like to sign up as well.

"Five hundred dollars for a class? That's way too expensive!" was the reply. Undeterred by his neighbor's response, Robert invested in the class and applied everything that he learned, ultimately leading to a massive fortune and the opportunity to turn around and teach others how to become rich as well. His neighbor continued to live the average life that he had always lived. Which cost more money in the long run? Investing in a $500 class or not investing in the class?

Imagine if Robert had fallen victim to the same trap and had allowed money to filter his decision to learn how to prosper from real estate. It would have cost him his entire fortune!

How many times has this shown up in your life? How many times have you been presented with an opportunity—maybe a class, a business venture, or simply a purchase that would ultimately lead you to greater fulfillment and enjoyment—but you turned it down because of the money? Remember the difference between those who are "interested" and those who are *committed*. "Interested" people allow things like money to stop them, while *committed* people find a way to make it happen. It all comes down to how much you value yourself and the things you desire to have in life. Regardless of the price, money can always be found if the value and the urgency are high enough. Let me give you an example.

In your success journal, write a description of your dream home. What does it look like? If you're like most people, it's probably a beautiful mansion with plenty of space for you and your family to enjoy all that life has to offer. What would a home like that cost? Depending on the location, probably somewhere in the millions, if not tens of millions of dollars. Now imagine that you meet someone who just so happens to be the owner of the exact home that you've always dreamed of. This person is at the age where he would like to retire and move away to a tropical paradise. You find out that he has always wanted to give someone an opportunity that he never received and will actually be selling his multimillion-dollar estate for just $50,000 as long as the buyer can pay cash up front for it within the next seven days. You end up doing a walk-through of the house and see that it is in pristine condition. You even have him draw up legal documents, show them to your attorney, and find out that the offer is 100 percent real. There's just one problem. You don't have $50,000 in your bank account. What would you do? Just like the scenario with the rich relative in Africa, if you're like most people, you would find a way to come up with the $50,000 and move into your dream home. Why? Because you saw the value in it.

The only reason anyone makes a purchase of any kind is because, at least in that moment, what they are purchasing has more intrinsic value than the money that they are trading for it. Everyone has access to money. Everyone. There are many who choose to limit themselves to what they can see right in front of them (these are typically the ones who use the phrase "I can't afford it . . ."), but those who achieve success know that there is *always* a way to obtain money or other resources if an opportunity presents itself and if they value the opportunity enough. When a person says, "I can't afford that . . . ," what he or she is really saying is, "I don't value that enough to trade money for what you are offering."

The problem arises when people don't value themselves, their education, or their results enough to invest in themselves. My friend, be *constantly* seeking out ways to further invest in yourself. Remember the mantra, "If it's right, what else matters?" Trust your heart, and when opportunities present themselves, take immediate action. Sign up for and attend seminars, purchase and read books, and value yourself enough so that when the time comes for others to invest in you through your products or services, they will feel the personal value emanating from you enough that they purchase your products or services. Remember, an investment in yourself is the greatest investment that you can make, and it can give you higher returns than any other investment.

Embarrassment

I was chosen out of all of the kids in my school district to be a member of the elite singing group during my fifth- and sixth-grade years. This group had it all! We had the flashy costumes, the fancy sound equipment, the bright lights, the dancers. We were known as the best elementary school performing group in all of Southern California. There was a part in the program that we had put together my sixth-grade year when the music featured a brief saxophone solo. For a bit of comic relief, I was chosen to run out from backstage when the solo began, dressed as a former US president with a real saxophone in my mouth, go down to my knees and pretend to play my heart out on that musical instrument. I had done this during countless performances and always elicited much welcomed laughter from the audience. I then showed up to a performance that we learned was going to be held outside on a raised cement platform. There were to be hundreds in attendance that day, and I wanted to show them the very best that I had to offer.

I had it all planned out. After putting on my costume and arming myself with that beautiful instrument, I was going to burst out from backstage, leap off the top cement step, land on the bottom step, go down to my knees and create the most magical moment these audience members had ever seen! And that is exactly what happened . . . with the exception of everything that happened after I burst out from backstage. As I went to do my leap, I tripped and began rolling, saxophone still in my mouth, down each step of the cement platform until I landed with a giant *thud* at the bottom. A groan of intense pain came screeching out of my mouth. Not only the entire audience but also all seventy-four other student performers in the group burst into a torrent of laughter. After moments of lying helplessly on the ground, I finally summoned the courage to scoop my battered carcass up off of the pavement and slowly hobble backstage.

While I can easily laugh at the incident now, it was one of the most embarrassing moments of my life then. I considered never singing again. I'm grateful that I didn't listen to that tempting inner voice that told me to quit, because I continued to sing and perform, which ultimately led me to some of the skills I would need to be where I am today.

Embarrassment is a very interesting emotion. Any time we feel embarrassed, a chemical is released in the brain that causes a very brief but very real physical sting that the body associates with death. We literally feel like we are about to die any time we are embarrassed, which is why we tend to be very reluctant to do things that cause us to move outside of our comfort zone. As you progress along the journey to success, you can be sure that your embarrassment button is going to be pushed. Do you remember the story of my first professional presentation and how scared I was that no one would sign up for my next-level class? What worried me the most was how embarrassing it would have been if not one single person had registered. That has actually happened to me on more than one occasion since then. You know what? It really was embarrassing, but I didn't let it stop me. It is incredibly tempting to curl up in a little ball and hide underneath the covers so as to never be seen again and, therefore, never feel the sting of embarrassment again.

The key to getting through the embarrassment filter is to spend as much time outside your comfort zone as possible. If you strongly fear public speaking and being in front of groups of people, spend time speaking in front of groups of people. If you are worried about the embarrassment of rejection, put yourself in situations where you might be rejected as often as you can. For example, if you are single and afraid of being rejected when you ask someone for a date, ask as many people as possible for a date. The purpose of this is to eventually grow your comfort zone to the point where those things are no longer embarrassing. Things are only embarrassing until they're not. I'll say that one more time. Things are only embarrassing until they're not. Eventually your comfort zone becomes large enough that things simply don't affect you the way they used to. Grow your comfort zone to ensure that embarrassment is no longer a filter in your life.

Judgment

How many times have you been judged or criticized? Judgment is possibly the most difficult filter to get through, because it requires total and complete self-acceptance regardless of what others say or think. Judgment can be especially difficult to overcome when it comes from those we love and care the most about. I love the phrase "Those that let their light shine brightest offend the most cockroaches." What can we do when this happens? Do we simply take it, keep our mouths shut, and do whatever is necessary to please the naysayers? Do we allow judgment to stop us in our tracks and keep us from moving forward? There are many who do give up. For them, reaching high levels of success and living their dreams simply isn't worth it if they encounter judgment and criticism along the way. Are there ways to deal with judgment and criticism in a positive way so that we are no longer affected?

The first step in overcoming judgment is to recognize when it has occurred in your life and what pattern it has taken. As I've looked back on my own life and pondered this subject, I've noticed a recurring set of events that form what I call my judgment cycle. It usually begins with me learning a skill.

One example was when I learned how to efficiently wait tables and got a job as a server in the city where I lived. I am usually a fast learner and have no problem working hard to improve myself. This would usually lead to me receiving praise and recognition from my supervisors as they saw my efforts. Their kind words always motivated me to work even harder and become the very best at whatever I was doing and, usually, I eventually did reach the top spot. This would almost certainly bring out feelings of jealousy toward me from my co-workers, who would then begin to judge, gossip, and spread rumors about me to each other as well as to my supervisors. I would inevitably lose the approval and recognition I once had from my supervisors, leading me to work even harder and do anything in my power to try to earn that approval back. This became exhausting, as it would seem like my efforts were in vain and nothing I did anymore was ever good enough. I would feel confused, frustrated, hurt, and depressed. Why bother trying if my efforts always went unnoticed? This cycle has repeated itself in various forms throughout my life.

Grab your success journal and write down the following steps in the judgment cycle.

1. Learn a skill
2. Receive praise and recognition from others, often from supervisors, parents, or other leaders
3. Strive to be the very best
4. Feelings of jealousy and judgment from associates, leading to backlash and backbiting
5. Loss of praise and recognition
6. Attempt to be even better to earn approval back
7. Failing to earn back approval, leading to feeling that no amount of effort is ever good enough
8. Confusion, frustration, hurt, and depression

Once you have this written down, ponder ways that the judgment cycle shows up in your life and then write them down. Yours may look different from mine. The important thing at this point is to find where your patterns begin so that you can change them from the early stages. But why do people judge and criticize in the first place?

A hotel clerk was once in the middle of a shift when a man, trying to check in, began to scream at the top of his lungs at the clerk over a problem that was obviously not his fault. After several minutes, the man finally left, allowing the next customer in line to step forward and check in. The clerk looked up at the new customer with just as big a smile as ever and, joyfully, asked how he could best serve him, as if nothing had ever happened. The new customer, confused, asked the clerk how he could withstand such degrading verbal abuse for so long and not have it affect him. "It's very simple," was the reply. "I wasn't the actual problem. He wasn't actually mad at me. I just happened to be the one he was taking his frustrations out on."

People have the tendency to see in others what they don't like about themselves. I call this the "mirror effect." People love to draw attention away from their own follies so as to pass the blame of whatever they are going through on to someone else. The flaws that they generally point out in other people are typically the flaws that they themselves struggle with.

Sometimes criticism comes from well-meaning people who simply jump to conclusions because they don't have all the facts. I remember the first time I told my family I was going to marry Heather, whom I had only met a few weeks earlier. This was before they had met her, so naturally they responded with skepticism and criticism. Once they finally met her and her family and saw just how perfect we were for each other, they warmed up to the idea.

Judgment often comes from simple misunderstandings. How many times have you ever taken someone's intentions to mean one thing when, in reality, they meant something totally different?

Criticism *always* follows those who set out to do some good in the world. Think back to the greatest men and women to ever walk the earth. They were hated and despised for what they accomplished. Whenever a force for good challenges forces of evil, forces of evil will do all they can to combat it. Think of Martin Luther King Jr. Here is a man who made more progress than possibly any other when it came to helping African Americans receive civil rights in the United States. He was ridiculed, thrown in jail, and eventually martyred for his cause.

If you are being ridiculed for trying to follow your heart, celebrate it! It likely means that you are on to something amazing, and forces of opposition are doing all that they can to counter it. Remember that those who let their light shine brightest offend the most cockroaches. Not everyone is going to like you, and that's OK! Be a force for good in the world, and don't you dare allow negativity to stop you! You are too precious and too valuable to do so!

It is also important to rid yourself of judgment toward others. Any time you judge or criticize someone, you then attract that same judgment or criticism into your own life. A wise man I knew once told me to strive to view other people and circumstances as neither good nor bad, but simply "are." For example, if someone cuts you off on the highway, try to view that situation as neither good nor bad; it simply happened. Does this take some practice? Absolutely. Our natural response is to get angry and take action to get even. But does this help? Do increased levels of stress hormones pumping through our systems really do us any good? Of course not. Remaining neutral and loving regardless of what happens can, however, do amazing things for us.

Here is an exercise that you can do if you truly want to implement this principle in your life. Be warned, though: this tool is only for those who are absolutely committed to creating massive results in their lives and doing everything it takes to get there. If that describes you, grab your success journal and create a list of absolutely everyone that you have ever judged or that you believe has ever judged you. This will probably turn out to be a pretty long list if you're anything like me. As you continue to add names, more and more will pop into your mind. Don't disregard them when they do. If they come to your mind, it's because they need to be on that list.

Once you feel that your list is complete, proceed to do a very intense emotional clearing technique that I have affectionately named the Gingerbread Man Exercise. You will need several pieces of scratch paper and a pen. Step one is to draw a rough outline of a person to represent the first name on your list, including a face at the top. This rough outline may resemble a gingerbread man, hence the name of the exercise. Write the person's name at the top. You now have a visual tool to use. Step two is to go to a place where you can be totally alone and not be disturbed or heard. Your car may be a good place for this, or a secluded field in nature. Then verbally ask the person, by name, for permission to fully express yourself to them. You will most likely hear a "yes" in your mind. Now you can proceed to step three, which is to tell that person absolutely everything you have ever wanted to say to them. If they were the one to judge you, tell them off. Hold nothing back. If you need to throw a tantrum and have a little "come-apart," go right ahead. You must get everything off your chest in order for this exercise to be effective, and you must do this *out loud.* Trying to do this exercise only in your mind will have the opposite effect and actually sink the negative emotions within you even deeper.

Once you have completed the *verbal* release of emotion, it is now time to proceed to step four, the *physical* release of emotion. Has there ever been a person in your life that you've always wished you could just slap or punch in the face? Here's your chance. Take the piece of paper in your hands and physically let all of your emotion out. You can slap it, punch it, rip its head off, throw it on the ground and stomp on it, whatever you need to do to release your emotions. This may bring up a lot of tears and, if so, wonderful. Let them come. This can be a very cleansing process.

Step five can often be the most difficult, but also the most important. Pick the paper back up (or the shredded pile of paper, if applicable) and ask for forgiveness for holding those feelings and emotions inside you. The words "Will you forgive me?" must leave your lips. As they do, you will likely feel a weight being lifted off your shoulders.

Finally, imagine that the person's greatest and highest self is standing in front of you or sitting beside you. Tapping into your intuition, speak the words out loud that you imagine his or her highest self would say to you in this moment. This could include an apology, words of gratitude, whatever comes to your mind. Speak them as if you were this person.

While this process can be very intense and quite time-consuming, as you go through your list one by one and get this done, few things are as cleansing and liberating. As you go through your list, go in order, person by person, without skipping anyone. Your subconscious put them in the order that they are in.

What do you do if, during step one when you ask for permission to express yourself, you hear a no in your mind? This is quite rare, but if it does happen, do not proceed. This person's spirit is not ready to hear what you have to say. Rather than express yourself verbally, write this person a letter and then tear it to shreds.

When you arrive at the name of a person whom you have judged, use step two to express your remorse for judging them. While their ears won't be able to hear the message, the person's spirit will be able to feel it. You may feel impressed at this point to talk to the person directly. If this happens, make sure to do it. This will be a huge part of your journey to success. Doing this exercise is how we remove our emotional *anchors*. Have you ever tried to go after a goal but felt as if you were being held down? It was probably because you had some emotional anchors keeping you in the same place. Do this exercise and cut those ties. Then place your hand over your heart and say, "I'm awesome!"

Now that you have removed judgment from your system, allow yourself to be filled with love toward yourself and others. When your entire being is filled with love, there is no room left for judgment. Love acts like a shield around you, protecting you from the effects of judgment and criticism. See yourself as the amazing person that you are and recognize your own positive characteristics. A great way to do this is to stand in front of the mirror every morning and tell your body just how much you love it. Grab your belly and say how beautiful it is. Rub your hands along your body and give yourself compliments. This not only helps you build confidence, but studies have shown that this can actually help your body to be healthier and function more efficiently.

What if the judgment comes from those closest to you? What do you do when you have a dream, take steps to pursue that dream, and you encounter opposition from members of your own family? One of my mentoring students encountered this in a fierce way. She had a dream of improving her life. When I first met her, she was bulimic, broke, constantly stressed, and simply afraid of exploring things beyond the boundaries that her parents had set for her. When she made the decision to invest in one of my mentoring programs, she experienced a major backlash from her family that she had never felt before. They told her how foolish she was for pursuing her dreams and "breaking the mold," so to speak, that her family had set. One of her sisters cut ties with her completely. This broke her heart. She loves her family so deeply and struggled with the idea that her choices didn't please them.

How many times have you experienced this? Have all of your loved ones always supported every decision you have ever made? Or have you experienced fierce opposition when you chose to pursue a different path than what was the norm in your family? When this happens, set clear boundaries. You deserve to be respected and treated with kindness. Don't let anyone, regardless of who they are, try to tell you otherwise. It is perfectly OK to limit the amount of time you spend with those who do nothing but bring you down. You have a mission in life. No one has the right to keep you from fulfilling that mission. Thankfully, my student followed her heart, continued to push through the rough times, and in less than a year, overcame her eating disorder, started making more than $10,000 per month, and married the man of her dreams.

I once read of a husband who was absolutely fed up with his wife's negativity. He loved her dearly and wanted to preserve the marriage, but her constant belittling and criticizing made keeping their relationship alive extremely difficult. They decided to see a marriage counselor, who suggested that, whenever she fell into a fit of negativity, he should politely excuse himself from the room. He would tell her, "I love you. I am leaving the room. I am not leaving the relationship." He set a clear personal boundary that meant that he would no longer listen to his wife's negativity, and it didn't take long for the problem to be resolved.

Grab your success journal and write down three personal boundaries you would like others to follow when they are around you. They could include such phrases as "Be respectful when talking to me," "No complaining while around me," "No gossiping around me," or whatever you wish. Once you have these rules set and written down, visualize yourself posting these rules around your personal space so that all who come in contact with you may feel their energy and know right away to follow them. Now place your hand over your heart and say, "I'm awesome!"

What do you do if the criticism persists? The truth is that some people can't be avoided completely and will simply have to be dealt with. You can't kick everyone out of your life, especially if it is your spouse or others that you live with who are judging you. If you are in this situation, surround yourself with people who love and support you as much as possible. You are the average of the five people you spend the most time with, so choose positive people to be your friends who will encourage you to follow your passions and your dreams.

Finally, realize that you aren't going to please everyone, no matter how hard you try. I recently read a quote that said:

> You are not for everyone. The world is filled with people who, no matter what you do, will point-blank not like you. But it is also filled with those who will love you fiercely. They are

your people. You are not for everyone, and that's OK. Talk to the people who can hear you.

Don't waste your precious time and gifts trying to convince them of your value. They won't ever want what you're selling. Don't convince them to walk alongside you. You'll be wasting both your time and theirs and will likely inflict unnecessary wounds, which will take precious time to heal. You are not for them and they are not for you. Politely wave them on and continue along your way. Sharing your path with someone is a sacred gift; don't cheapen this gift by rolling yours in the wrong direction.—Author unknown

When you encounter opposition, celebrate it! You are probably on the right track and are doing some good in the world. Make sure that, deep down, you are enough regardless of what other people say and do. It will be this confidence that helps attract wealth to you.

CHAPTER 5:

BECOMING WEALTHY

Have you ever known someone who keeps attracting the same circumstances into their life? Maybe they keep getting the same kind of dead-end job or the same type of relationships. Perhaps they're always broke at the end of the month regardless of how much money they earn. Have you ever heard of anyone who sets out to become wealthy, starts a business, works long hours, does everything that they know to do, but ends up bankrupt? Have you ever heard of someone who may be a total schmuck with no formal education who starts a business and is an instant success? What are the differences between those who make it financially and those who don't?

T. Harv Eker, author of *Secrets of the Millionaire Mind* and the genius whose teachings the majority of this chapter will be based on, explains that it all begins with what he calls a person's *financial thermostat.* Think of a regular thermostat. If you walk into a room that is 72 degrees, it is pretty likely that the thermostat in that room is set at 72 degrees. You could open a door or window and allow some air to enter the room to raise or lower the temperature by a few degrees, but eventually that thermostat is going to kick on and drive that room right back to 72 degrees. It's the same when it comes to money.

How many lottery winners have you heard of that were just as broke a few years later as they were before they won? This is because, even though they amassed a large fortune, their financial thermostats were still set very low. Contrast that with a gentleman I'm sure you've heard of who goes by the name of Donald Trump. Trump is a multi-billion-aire who has actually lost everything he had on multiple occasions. Since his financial thermostat was set for billions, each time he lost his money he had it all back and then some within a few short years.

How can you know where your thermostat is set? It's simple: just take a look at your current financial results. If you are like millions of people who have been banging their heads against the wall trying to figure out why your financial situation is going nowhere, it is probably because your thermostat is not set any higher than the amount of money you are currently receiving. If your financial thermostat is not set for high levels of success, large amounts of money will probably never come to you. Thankfully, there is hope. Regardless of what your thermostat is set for, there are steps that you can take, starting right now, to change it.

As always, the first step when it comes to change is awareness. Eker further explains that each person's financial thermostat is usually formed during childhood from three main things:

1) What you heard about money:

If you grew up in a home that was anything like mine, you prob-ably heard all of the clichés like "money doesn't grow on trees," "money can't buy happiness," "money is the root of all evil," etc. Let's use that last one as an example. If you are indoctrinated with the idea that having money will make you evil, what will you do, possibly without even realizing it, when you get money?

2) What you saw regarding money:

What was your parents' relationship with money as you were growing up? Did they have a positive or a negative relationship with it? Were your parents good at managing money or were they frivolous with it? Did you ever walk in on your parents arguing about money or complaining about having to pay bills? All of these affect our financial thermostat.

3) What you experienced with money:

There was a young nurse who went through one of Eker's programs who wanted to figure out why her financial state was where it was. She made good money as a nurse but could never seem to hang on to it. She was completely broke at the end of each month and couldn't figure out what to do about it. She recalled having an experience when she was eight years old. Her parents took her out to a fancy Chinese restaurant, and when the bill for the meal came, her mother and father began a bitter, heated argument over money and the cost of the expensive meal. Her father, enraged, stood up to storm out of the restaurant, when he collapsed right there at the table from a heart attack. At eight years old, this girl was on her community's swim team and jumped down to administer CPR to her father. But he died right there in her arms. From that moment on, she subconsciously associated money with the feelings of pain and death, so naturally she got rid of money each time she got it.

Get your success journal out and answer the following questions:
1. What I heard about money growing up was . . .
2. What I saw regarding money growing up was . . .
3. What I experienced with money growing up was . . .

This information can be used to help you identify your exact financial thermostat and then begin to change it.

The next step is to recognize the differences between the actions of poor or middle-class people and those who are extremely wealthy.

Many poor or middle-class people have the mindset that "life happens to me." They say things like, "Oh, getting rich just isn't in the cards for me," or "I am just trying to make the most out of the hand that life dealt me." They believe that they are victims of their circumstances and that there is little or nothing that can be done to change their circumstances. Rich and successful people, on the other hand, understand that they are the creators of their lives and take full responsibility for their circumstances. If there is something they don't like about their lives, they go to work to change it.

Many poor and middle-class people complain about their lives and then justify their circumstances while blaming others or the economy. They say things like, "Rich people all cheated the system or did something dishonest to get to where they are," or "Why would I want to be rich? The government will just take it all away anyway." Rich and successful people, again, take full responsibility for their lives. If there is something that they don't think is working for them, they either change it or figure out a way to make it work.

Many poor and middle-class people think in terms of "either-or." "Either I can be rich or I can spend time with my family." "I can either be wealthy or spiritual." "I can either be successful or honest." The rich and successful have a "both" mentality. "I can be both rich *and* spiritual." "I can be wealthy *and* spiritual." "I can be successful *and* honest."

Many poor and middle-class people are selfish with their time and means. Each year, one of the restaurants I used to work for took an entire month and raised money to donate to a children's hospital that provided free care to its patients and was run entirely off of donations. As a server, I had the opportunity to let every guest know of the fundraiser we were doing and tell them that, while there was certainly no obligation to do so, they could donate $1 or more to help children in need. It shocked me when the majority of my guests responded that they couldn't afford to donate $1 because of their own meager circumstances. Most of those who responded in this way had also ordered the most expensive items on the menu, pricey beverages, appetizers, and desserts. However, many rich and successful people understand the principle of karma and generously give away a large percentage of their earnings to help those less fortunate.

Many poor and middle-class people resent the rich and successful. Who do you think coined the phrase "filthy rich," a poor person or a wealthy person? The rich tend to be among the most highly judged and criticized. How many times have you heard someone complain about the 1% "hoarding all the money"? What they don't realize is that by resenting, judging, and criticizing those with wealth, they are almost guaranteeing that they will never have wealth and success. If they ever did, they would become the very thing that they resent, judge, and criticize. Rich people, on the other hand, admire and model other rich people. They associate with those who are at a similar or higher economic status and use that association to learn from each other how to maintain and grow their wealth.

Many poor and middle-class people think they already know everything there is to know about success and, if there is something they don't know, they believe they can figure everything out themselves. They scoff at the idea of paying money to attend a seminar or hire a coach to help them reach their goals. Rich people always have a mentor. They realize that they don't know everything and are constantly seeking to improve their skills. They understand that their mind is their greatest asset and regularly invest in ways to continue to develop it.

Many poor and middle-class people make money the primary factor in decision making. How many times have you seen something you desired but had to ask the price before deciding whether or not to purchase it? For rich people, cost is still factored in, but it isn't the primary factor. They base their purchases on value, not just on cost. They don't allow money to govern their decisions.

Many poor and middle-class people are poor at managing money. They might be frivolous spenders and get themselves deeper and deeper into bad debt each month. They might be money hoarders and reject every investment opportunity that comes their way. They might be money avoiders and dislike the idea of even using money in the first place. Successful people and those who get and stay rich tend to be excellent money managers. They understand that the better they manage their money, the more money they can receive.

Notice that I didn't say that the rich *budget* their money. Cut that word out of your vocabulary! A budget comes from a mindset of scarcity. It essentially means that there is a very finite amount of money that can be created and an even smaller amount of money that can be spent or enjoyed. This is fine if you want to stay poor or middle-class, but no one has ever budgeted their way to great wealth. A money management system, on the other hand, allows for unlimited earning and creating potential, which brings us to our final comparison. Many poor and middle-class people live below their means. Rich people expand their means. They never limit what they can earn or create. If they see something they desire, they make it happen. Period.

Why is it that good money managers tend to have more money? Imagine for a moment that you own multiple restaurants and assign a general manager to each one. As time progresses, are you more likely to promote and give stewardship over more restaurants to the good managers or the not-so-good managers? The same concept is true with money. I like to imagine that there is a stewardship department in the sky that blesses us with less money if we are poor money managers and more if we are good money managers.

But if we aren't supposed to use a budget, what other systems can be used to manage our money? In Feel Well, Live Well, we assign all our students to use what we call the Becoming Wealthy System. This is a foolproof method of managing your money. You start by going to your bank or credit union and opening up several sub-accounts or savings accounts until you have a total of six different accounts, and then you give them the following names: Essentials, Generosity, Education, Financial Freedom Fund, Wealth Accumulation Account, and Celebration. Each time you receive money, you divide it among the accounts in the following manner:

50% into Essentials
10% into Generosity
10% into Education
10% into Financial Freedom Fund
10% into Wealth Accumulation Account
10% into Celebration

Your Essentials account is used just like a regular checking account to pay for all of your necessities, such as your house, your car, gas, groceries, utilities, etc. The money in Generosity is given to charity. If you belong to a church that practices tithing, that would come out of this account. If not, simply find a great charity to give 10% of your income. The next 10% of your income then goes toward furthering your education, whatever that may mean to you. The most successful people who ever lived constantly improved their minds, so you now have a fund to put toward attending seminars, purchasing books and audio trainings, hiring mentors, and so forth. The next 10% will go toward investing in passive income strategies, such as real estate. Notice that Education comes before this, because it is critical to learn how to become a successful investor from those who have done it before venturing into that realm yourself. Once you do, you will have a decent amount of capital saved up in your Financial Freedom Fund. This account is *not* for paying off debt. That comes from your Essentials. The money in your Financial Freedom Fund (or FFF) is *never* to be spent, only invested. Your Wealth Accumulation

Account (or WAA) is used like a savings account and, just as the name implies, it is used to grow your net worth. Finally, your Celebration account is a way to practice what it is like to be wealthy. This account must be blown in its entirety every single month on experiences that help to put you into an abundance mindset. This means that every month you have an excuse to go to the nicest restaurant you can think of, or stay at the nicest hotel, or spend a day at the nicest spa in town. This is done, once again, to practice being wealthy, because practice makes permanent. If you practice living like a pauper your entire life, it's pretty likely you will forever be a pauper. If you practice celebrating the things in life that you are grateful for by living like a king or queen for a day each month, it's a lot more likely that you will reach a point where you will live like a king or queen *every* day of each month. No, this is not frivolity. This is a way to nurture yourself and help yourself visualize, through experience, the process of being wealthy.

What if 50% of your income won't cover all of your essentials? What if you are like the unfortunate majority, who can barely scrape by with 100% of their earnings going toward paying for their basic needs? The key to this system is that the *habit* is more important than the *dollar amount*. I'll say that one more time. The *habit* is more important than the *dollar amount*. This means that if you need to start small and divide just $1 each month, placing 50 cents into your Essentials account and 10 cents into each of the others, you do so. Each month you take the 10 cents from your Celebration account, buy a small piece of candy, and enjoy the heck out of it! Then maybe the next month you can divide $2, and then $4, and so forth, until you are able to get by on 50% of your income going toward your essentials. I cannot tell you how many testimonials I have received from my students and clients who have incorporated this system into their lives and have seen a massive difference, almost like magic, simply because they are now excellent managers and stewards over money.

Get out your success journal and write down the Becoming Wealthy System. Then take action and begin to incorporate it immediately. Now place your hand over your heart and say, "I'm awesome!"

Now that you understand the importance of managing your money well, let's clarify a few money misconceptions. These are ideas that you may be quite familiar with and may even be practicing. These are concepts that may work for middle-class people, but hanging on to these beliefs will limit how far you can progress financially.

Misconception #1: Live below your means. There is an extremely expensive phrase in the English language which too many people use: "I can't afford it." Saying or even thinking this phrase is one of the most financially damaging things that you can do to yourself. This allows your brain to be lazy and cuts off possibilities of making things happen. Simply turning it around to "How can I afford it?" puts your brain to work and allows you to expand your means and grow your wealth.

Misconception #2: Cut up your credit cards. This is counsel that many grandparents give to their newlywed grandchildren. This may be good counsel for a poor person who is overly frivolous whenever they have a credit card, but this immediately eliminates most of your opportunities to invest in yourself. Most investment opportunities require good credit, and there aren't many ways to build good credit without a credit card. This leads us to our next misconception.

Misconception #3: Avoid debt like the plague. There is a huge difference between good debt and bad debt. Bad debt is an expense that takes money out of your pocket, such as consumer debt, education that you don't use, and so forth. Yes, education can definitely fall under the category of bad debt if you don't use it to create a return on your investment. How many people do you know who spent years in college pursuing a degree that they don't use? Now they have thousands and thousands of dollars that they must pay back for a piece of paper with their name on it hanging on the wall. Good debt, or *loans*, means using someone else's money to put more money into your pocket. Education that you do use is a great example. If you go to school to become an attorney, for example, and then take that education to create a very successful law practice, that education falls into the category of a loan, or good debt. For me, hiring personal mentors was a fantastic use of good debt. I borrowed tens of thousands of dollars from banks and credit unions to hire the best mentors I could find, and then used what they taught me to create an enormous return on that investment over and over and over again. While many middle-class people view debt as a crushing weight that they desperately want to remove, the wealthy use loans like a platform to get ahead financially.

Think of it this way. Let's say you make $2,000 a month, and that what you owe in credit card fees, personal loans, etc., is $10,000. Let's say that your expenses are $1,500 per month, leaving you with $500. What most middle-class people tend to do is put the entire $500 toward paying down the $10,000 debt. Think about that for a moment. If you were paying $500 toward a $10,000 debt, you would need to be paid twenty times to pay the entire amount off, not factoring in any interest. Now let's say you do what a lot of wealthy (or soon-to-be wealthy) people do and pay only the minimum payment of $100 toward your loans each month for a certain period of time, leaving you with $400 to invest each month. Let's say you also take out a few extra loans to invest in assets, hire a personal mentor to teach you new skills, and that you start applying these new skills over a twelve-month period. Now, rather than owing $10,000, you owe $40,000, but rather than making only $2,000 a month, you make $50,000 a month. Let's assume that your expenses are now $5,000 per month, leaving you with a cash flow of $45,000 per month. Even though what you owe is now significantly higher, your income is also much higher, and you could pay off everything you owe in a single month.

Obviously this is all hypothetical, but this is how successful people think. It is 100 percent OK to borrow money to put toward assets that will help you earn more money, including your greatest asset: your mind. If you want to be rich, you've got to act as rich people do.

Misconception #4: If I get rich, someone else is getting poorer. This comes from the misconception that there is a finite amount of resources in the world and, like a big pie, if one person has more, that must mean that others get less. This couldn't be further from the truth. The truth is that this planet is extremely *rich* in resources and money. It was once calculated that if all the money in the world were divided equally among every person on the planet, every single person would be a millionaire. Learn to be a good receiver when money and other good things come to you. When someone offers you money for something, graciously accept and put it into your pocket. Each time you come across a coin on the ground, pick it up and celebrate the fact that life just sent you some money. Not doing so sends a message to your subconscious that you don't want money, so why would money come to you?

Misconception #5: Money is the root of all evil. This is most often heard among spiritual individuals. What is ironic is that most of the greatest men and women to ever live whose lives are recorded in the scriptures were quite rich. If money was the root of all evil, why did God choose rich people to lead His people? Money is neutral. It's what you do with it that determines whether good things or not-so-good things come of it. I like to tell people that if money is the root of all evil, then my pencil is the root of all misspelled words. In fact, the saying "Money is the root of all evil" is a misconception itself, since the Bible actually says, "The *love* of money is the root of all evil" (1 Timothy 6:10, emphasis added).

Misconception #6: Save, Save, Save! A few short years ago when I hit my lowest-ever financial point, I asked a trusted associate for help and assistance. He agreed and got me the help that I needed to get food for my family and keep a roof over our heads. Months later, once my business had taken a turn for the better, he congratulated me for my success and gave me the advice to stash away any and all extra earnings that I made after paying for my basic needs. Saving money is certainly a principle of success (and after all, 10% of one's income goes into a Wealth Accumulation Account), but no one, not one single person, has ever saved themselves to extreme wealth, because money stagnant is money wasted. I understood the power of investing, at least on a very basic level, and knew that if the opportunity presented itself to invest some of my extra earnings into creating even larger earnings, I was going to take it. Doing so has proven to make all the difference for me. "But Eric, aren't we supposed to save money for a 'rainy day'?" That would depend on how many "rainy days" you hope to have. Remember that whatever you focus on and put energy toward eventually manifests itself in your life, so if you purposely set money aside for emergencies, you'll probably attract some emergencies. If you put money aside for fantastic days, like vacations or special occasions, you'll probably attract more fantastic days, vacations, and special occasions. What do you want life to give you? You get to decide.

Get out your success journal and something to write with. Answer the following questions: The money misconceptions that I have had are . . . These are affecting my financial results in the following ways . . . To overcome this, I will . . .

Now place your hand over your heart and say, "I'm awesome!"

CHAPTER 6:

RELATIONSHIPS

took a major leap of faith when I first opened my healthcare practice. I had just been certified as a practitioner of B.E.S.T., the Bio-Energetic Synchronization Technique, and was looking forward to finally being able to quit my full-time job waiting tables and focus on doing what I loved. I pictured myself growing a large, lucrative practice so that the transition would be painless and without financial worry when it came time to quit my full-time job. Fortunately, or unfortunately, it didn't work out quite the way I had planned. I had been praying for several months to know when the best time would be to hand in my notice. That day came much sooner than expected.

July 31, 2013, was my final day in the restaurant industry. I will never forget turning in my serving apron and clocking out for the final time. What was to become of me? I hadn't been able to grow a steady income with B.E.S.T.; I didn't even have a place to practice. I was jumping into deep water with nothing but a determination to swim.

I found a suitable space within a few weeks inside an existing chiropractic office and announced to all of my friends and family that I was open for business. I just knew that I would be making large amounts of money in no time at all. There was just one problem; that was the main outcome I was hoping for, and the fact that I no longer had a steady stream of income with which I could support my family didn't make matters any easier. I began to view people as walking dollar signs and would think of ways that I could get as much money as possible out of their wallets and into mine to buy groceries and pay for the house we were living in. Do you think there's a small chance that people can pick up on the intentions of our hearts? Absolutely!

Because my mind was focused on making money rather than helping and serving people, my small clientele began to slowly dwindle and disappear. After only four months, I hit the lowest financial point of my life and was forced to go on welfare. How could this happen to me? I had never struggled to provide for my family, and now I was struggling to even put food on the table.

I didn't find the answer until a mentor of mine pointed out that our thoughts and feelings give off a certain energy which can be felt and interpreted by those around us. My clients could feel the fact that I was focused on money, so naturally they stopped coming in. I decided to try an experiment. From then on, each time I was with a client or a potential client, I would think in my mind, "You are amazing. You are absolutely incredible. You can achieve anything you desire. I would love to serve you in any way possible."

The results were like magic. My clientele doubled in one month alone, and my income quintupled within four months. Could it really be as easy as changing our thoughts as we interact with each other? Try this technique from now on. Any time you are with someone, focus on sending them compliments in your mind. You may be shocked at how much of a difference it can make in your relationships and overall results.

This is an exercise that you can even try remotely. Remember, our thoughts and emotions are all made of up energy, and energy knows no boundaries. I tried this once with a particular gentleman that I desperately needed to contact. He would never answer his phone, no matter how many times I called him. One day I thought I would try an experiment, and I sent him compliments in my mind as I dialed his number. To my surprise, he answered the phone! Was this merely a coincidence? If this had been a one-time occurrence, I would be tempted to say yes. But this has happened to me many times since as I have gone to call people on the phone or knock on someone's door. Other people can feel the positive energy emanating from you on a subconscious level. Since people are naturally drawn to things that make them feel good, they are much more likely to pick up the phone or answer the door. Does it happen every time? No, but it certainly increases your chances that you will get a positive response.

Our relationships play a major role in the levels of success that we achieve. If our major relationships are out of order, there will eventually come a time when we hit plateaus. These major relationships include those with ourselves, our Higher Power, money, food, our parents, our spouse, and others. Take a moment right now and get your success journal out and rate yourself from 1 to 10, with 10 being the highest, on how you are doing with each of those relationships. Be totally honest. This may be a good eye-opener for you. Once you've done this, answer the following journal prompt: "The reason each of my relationships are the way they are is that . . ."

The state of our relationships boils down to *emotion*, or *energy in motion*. Whatever kind of energy we are setting in motion toward our relationships will determine the kind of relationships we have, beginning from our initial greeting.

Toward the beginning of one of my seminars called Celebration of Relationships and Romance, I have all the participants go around the room and greet each other as if they can't stand anyone they meet and as if everyone else is a complete waste of space. They then greet everyone as if they are horribly afraid of rejection and they *have* to have everyone like them. Finally, they greet everyone as if they are their long-lost best friend. Some are shocked to notice the difference in the feelings that they get from everyone else as they play along through each of the exercises. Try practicing this among your family or friends. Feel the difference in the energy that you get from each person and use this experience to become more aware of the energy that you give off as you meet with people in your own life.

There are major differences between successful and unsuccessful relationships.

In unsuccessful relationships:
1) Individuals enter into the relationship simply to "check it out." Before I married Heather, several of my co-workers told me that we needed to live together for a time before getting married to make sure that we would be compatible. This seems to be a growing trend among young couples. What they don't realize is that, statistically speaking, this doubles the couple's chances of a failed relationship, because the couple enter the relationship without a firm commitment to each other. Once hardship or difficulty arises, couples like this tend to separate.
2) Each person places the responsibility of his or her individual happiness on the other person. It is up to the partner to "make them" happy, and they often set unrealistic expectations that the other partner can't meet.
3) Individuals enter into the relationship with emotional wounds, hoping the other will "heal" them. They hope their new partner will fill the emotional void that they have and, again, often set unrealistic expectations that the new partner can't meet.
4) Individuals are selfish and only focus on their individual needs.

On the other hand, in successful relationships:
1) Individuals allow their selfish needs to die. This doesn't mean that they don't take care of themselves and allow their basic

needs to be met; it simply means letting go of selfish, ego-driven habits.

2) Failure is not an option. Both individuals are in it for the long haul and make the relationship work no matter what.

3) Individuals are self-aware and work on healing and solving their own issues from the past. They understand that they are responsible for their own happiness.

4) Individuals are aware of their role in the relationship and execute it daily. This may mean different things to different people. The key here is to communicate openly with each other and see what expectations are there.

5) Individuals recognize their own egotistical tendencies and constantly strive to tame their EGO.

The EGO is an interesting thing. EGO is an acronym which stands for Edging God (and others) Out. You can always tell you are going into EGO when you become that really scary, nasty person that all of us become from time to time. The key is to *manage* or *tame* the EGO, not kill it, as many mistakenly try to do, because there is positive EGO and negative EGO. The negative creates a sense of separation between ourselves and others. When we are in this mode, we tend to want to feed our EGOs more than our relationships. Our negative EGOs tend to want to be right all the time and don't want to listen to things that contradict our ways of thinking. It labels things as "better than" or "worse than," judges and criticizes, and it clings to things outside of ourselves as if they were a part of our identity. Money is a great example of this. How many times have you or someone you know felt like you were a success or a failure depending on how much money was in the bank?

On the other hand, the positive EGO is what drives and motivates us to keep moving forward. It allows us to stand up to opposition and conquer our fears. Again, it's important to bridle or tame the EGO in order to have successful relationships. This can be achieved by first recognizing when you are going into EGO. Allow yourself to become aware of what triggers you and when your triggers happen. The first step to change is awareness. Allow yourself to focus on what is actually happening. The fact may be that someone just cut you off on the freeway. Rather than making it "right" or "wrong" in your mind, see it as simply what it is. Most people tend to make up stories in their minds that the person who just cut them off is a jerk or highly inconsiderate. They allow themselves to become angry, thus their negative EGO takes over. Again, when things like this happen to you, see the situation for what it is, but not more than what it is. Use nonjudgmental observations and allow things to simply "be."

What are your personal triggers? Grab your success journal right now and journal on the following: I go into negative EGO when . . .

What did this bring to your attention? Again, remember that the first step to change is awareness, and what you can see, you can change. Share this with a loved one and set a clear course of action to help correct this area in your life. Then place your hand over your heart and say, "I'm awesome!"

Guidelines for Happy Relationships

I was 17 years old the day my family life changed forever. I came home from an evening college class to see my parents sitting at the table with a man I had never seen before. He was wearing a dark suit and had a solemn look on his face. I paid it no mind and headed to my room to relax and watch some TV. About an hour went by when I heard a knock on my door. "Your mother and I need to talk to you," my dad explained. I followed him into the living room and sat down.

"Here's the deal, son. Your mother and I are getting a divorce and are selling the house. We need to be out of the house within the next thirty days." I was completely shocked! I had always known that my parents didn't exactly have what one would call a happy marriage, and I knew that separation would happen at some point. I just wasn't prepared for it when it finally occurred. What had happened between them? Why, after decades of marriage, was it suddenly ending this way?

I will also never forget the day that I married my sweetheart. Everything was so perfect. Heather and I arrived at a particular religious edifice in San Diego, California, the very city where I had been born 22 years earlier. This place was one of great significance to me. I had dreamed about getting married there for years, and the day had finally arrived.

Inside this building is a white staircase with a gold handrail. With both of us dressed in white, I took Heather by the hand and ascended this beautiful staircase to the room where we would be married for all eternity. I knelt down across from her at the altar and heard those beautiful words and blessings pronounced upon us as we became husband and wife. I looked into her gorgeous hazel eyes that were so full of love and thought that life simply couldn't get any better.

What was the difference between our relationship on the day of our wedding and my parents' relationship on the day that their marriage ended? Time is an obvious answer, but is there more to it than that? Over the years that we have been married, my wife and I have created a number of rules that have not only helped keep our marriage relationship strong but also our relationships in all areas of life.

Our first rule is simple: No dumping! How many times has a friend or family member used you to vent their frustrations about something that happened to them? How did that make you feel? If you're like most people, you would probably say that it didn't feel very good. During our first few years of marriage, whenever Heather and I would get upset at each other, we would spend hours spewing our emotions over each other until we finally found the root cause that made us upset in the first place. This process would usually last late into the night, causing us to be tired and resentful the next day. Now that we know a little more than we used to, whenever one of us becomes upset, we first release our emotions in private so that we can then share our feelings when we come together. Let me say that again. We release our *emotions* so that we can then share our *feelings*. No, these two words are not synonymous, as many mistakenly think they are. An emotion is the energy created by a particular feeling which leads to a physical process that takes place in the body. Our negative emotions can cloud our judgment and lead us into negative EGO, which is why it is important to release that energy before expressing your feelings to the person you need to talk to.

There are several great ways to do this. One of them is journaling. Grabbing a piece of paper and writing down everything that is on your mind is a great way to release emotion. Being able to express yourself freely on that paper is not only effective but also therapeutic. Another method is expressing yourself verbally in private to an inanimate object, such as a pillow or a steering wheel (your car is a great place to do this, because it's unlikely anyone else will hear you and you have a degree of privacy). Go ahead and vent all you want to these objects. Yell, scream, throw things, shake your fist in the air, get all of that negative energy out of you until you feel a weight lifted off your shoulders. Inanimate objects won't be harmed by your energy, but other people can be. People are not for dumping, and that includes social media. How many friends do you know who, seemingly every time they post something on social media, do so to vent a frustration? Any time you dump your negative emotions where someone else can hear or see them, that negative energy now affects them, which can cause major damage to relationships, both in the short and long term. Say the following out loud, "People are not for dumping!" Release your emotions in private so that you can then share your feelings.

Once you've done this or a similar exercise, you are then free to discuss your feelings with the other person, if you still need to. You may find that releasing your emotions is all that you needed, but if you still feel there is more to resolve, go ahead and talk with the person at this point. When my wife and I do this, since we have already removed our emotions, it usually doesn't take more than a few minutes to express our feelings, find a solution, give each other a hug and kiss, and go on with our day. Doesn't that sound easier than arguing for hours into the night?

Another critical element to any relationship is forgiveness. This is important when it comes to your relationship with yourself as well. You are human, imperfect, and make mistakes just like everyone else. Holding on to grudges is one of the worst things that you can do and will ultimately stunt your growth in at least one, if not many, areas of your life.

I can always tell when I have a patient on the table who holds grudges. It usually manifests itself in the form of back pain, neck pain, or abdominal pain. With B.E.S.T., I can usually help a patient get relief within about 60 seconds of beginning the treatment, unless they have unresolved issues with relationships. I had a particular patient when I was first starting my practice who had unrelenting back pain. She had tried everything: traditional chiropractic, massage therapy, and more, and nothing had given her lasting relief. After several minutes of treating her with B.E.S.T. and not seeing any change in her symptoms, I finally asked her, "Is there someone in your life that you need to forgive?" Her eyes got really wide, and she responded, "What if I'm not ready to forgive him yet?" I poked on the painful spots as hard as I could, to which she screamed out in pain, and I asked her,

"Is holding on to that really worth it? Because this pain that you are experiencing is the direct result of your grudge." She admitted that it wasn't worth it, and I walked her through the steps of forgiveness, after which her pain was gone.

Forgiveness is not about accepting or condoning the actions of another person. It doesn't mean you have to continue to have the same type of relationship with the other person as you did before. It simply means ridding yourself of the negative emotion that stems from whatever incident occurred. True forgiveness includes four critical steps:

Step 1) Release toxic emotion. Pretend that an inanimate object is the person involved, and tell that person off. Allow yourself to say everything you've always wanted to say to that person. You could also write a letter to the person that you don't ever send, or you could go to a place where you can be totally alone and allow yourself to throw a tantrum.

Step 2) Forgive yourself. This can be the hardest part of the process, but it is so important if lasting healing is to take place. Stop beating yourself up over what happened. Doing so doesn't help the situation. If restitution needs to take place, go and get it done, but then allow yourself to love yourself again. A great exercise to do is to stand in front of the mirror as you are getting ready for the day, rub your hands gently all over your body, and tell yourself good things. There is scientific evidence that suggests that doing this not only helps you to build personal confidence but also helps your body function better as it absorbs all of the positive energy you are giving it.

Step 3) Allow the other person to forgive you. This process may require that you ask them for forgiveness directly and make things right in the relationship. Sometimes this can take place during step 1 as you are releasing emotion and venting to the person's spirit. Once you feel as if you have expressed all that you need to express, allow the words "Will you forgive me?" to leave your lips.

Step 4) Learn the lesson and see the good in the situation. I am a firm believer that good can come from absolutely anything. Some situations are more difficult to see than others, but if you look hard enough, you can learn some sort of lesson in absolutely any situation.

Remember, forgiveness is for you, not for the other person. An old cliché says that holding on to a grudge is like drinking poison and hoping it kills the other person. It only causes damage to you and to your results.

The *Law of Indirect* says that the state of our relationships will eventually manifest itself in our success or lack thereof. Think about this for a moment. If your goal is to improve your health, you must first improve your relationship with yourself. If you want to improve your income, you need to improve your relationships with other people, since money comes from other people.

Let's start with your relationship with yourself. Dr. M. T. Morter Jr., developer of the Bio-Energetic Synchronization Technique and founder of Morter Health System, taught that there are six essential choices when it comes to taking care of ourselves:

1) What we eat
2) What we drink
3) What we breathe
4) How we exercise
5) How we rest
6) What we think

If you struggle with eating a healthy diet, begin to make small changes today. Add more fruits and vegetables to your diet, reduce the amount of refined sugars and flours you eat, avoid alcoholic drinks, and limit carbonated beverages. Focus on alkalizing your body through proper supplementation and drinking plenty of water. Get fresh air by spending time in nature, exercise regularly, and get plenty of rest at night.

While all of these are important, Dr. Morter explained that the most important area of focus is what we think. Remember that our thoughts are made up of energy and can actually help us become healthier or sicker, depending on what we tend to focus on. Have you ever known a family in which it seems as if someone is always sick? Do you think there's a pretty good chance that there may be what we like to call "stinkin' thinkin'" going on inside that family?

If you want your health to improve, start by focusing on the things that you like about yourself, even if it's something as simple as "I'm still breathing." Find things each day that you are thankful and grateful for, and focus your energy on those things. Whatever you focus on expands, so the more you are thankful and grateful, the more you receive to be thankful and grateful for. The more you show gratitude toward yourself and your body, the more you heal and nurture your soul.

Next, it is absolutely critical to clean up your relationship with your Higher Power. It doesn't matter to me what you call your Higher Power. I call mine God or Heavenly Father, but you can call yours whatever you wish. Don't have a Higher Power? Get one. They're free. If your relationship with your Higher Power is tainted because of things in your life that you need to clean up, you are cutting yourself off from your source of inspiration and guidance. Regardless of how much your EGO would like to take credit for your wins and successes, it was first your Higher Power that inspired you with ideas of actions to take to achieve those wins and successes. Do whatever is necessary to get those things cleaned up in your life. Talk to your local religious leader if you have one, make prayer and meditation a regular part of your daily routine, spend time in nature, and allow yourself to simply *be*. Your Higher Power knows quite a few more people in the world than you do, so by freeing up that channel of inspiration you are allowing yourself to receive guidance on how to get in touch with those people who can bring money and resources into your life.

Many people make the mistake of going after money and resources first. This is like trying to swim upstream in a raging river; it simply doesn't work. If you feel yourself getting stuck on a plateau in any area of success, take a close look at your life and where these relationships are. I bet there is at least one of these relationships that can be put back in order. Doing so may just clear up the energy required to bring those results to a new level.

I experienced this firsthand when I was getting started with my business. I mentioned that I took a leap of faith and quit my full-time job before I even had an office for my practice. The very next day after my final shift waiting tables, I drove to Southern California to meet with a family member with whom my relationship had fallen by the wayside. It took several hours, but we finally came to terms with each other, hugged, and wished each other the best. I strongly believe that doing so helped me to find an office and start my practice as quickly as I did, notwithstanding the fact that it took a few months to get off the ground.

Get your success journal back out. Make a list of all the relationships that you need to get in order, and then set a plan of action for making it happen. Now place your hand over your heart and say, "I'm awesome!"

Being Broke Sucks, So Stop It!

CHAPTER 7:

THE ART OF PERSUASION

worked for some time in a Brazilian steakhouse, or churrasca-ria. These restaurants are different from traditional steakhouses where you order your favorite cut of steak, tell them how you would like them to cook it, and have a server bring it to you on a plate with side dishes. In a Brazilian steakhouse, you get to eat all the meat you want.

Once you are seated at your table, a server will stop by and take your beverage order. They will direct you to a buffet in the middle of the restaurant with salads, soups, potatoes, rice, rolls, pastas, and other tasty side dishes. Then, every few minutes, a meat server will stop by your table with a different kind of meat, such as grilled sirloin, filet mignon, broiled salmon, and fried chicken wings, and ask you if you would like some. You may have as much or as little as you would like and may eat until you couldn't possibly eat any more.

At the restaurant where I worked, there were a number of items that were not included in the regular meat rotation but could be pur-chased for an additional charge, such as grilled shrimp, scallops, and 10-ounce lobster tails. Very few servers sold the latter; lobster tails cost an additional $30 on top of the $22 each person paid to dine there. In fact, most servers sold an average of only one or two lobster tails per year simply because they had the mindset that no one would want to spend that much money ordering something extra when they were already paying for more food than they could possibly eat.

Fortunately, my wife had recently attended a training where a gentleman named Tom Schreiter promised to teach all who were in attendance five words that could change their lives forever. After she passed this information on to me and I implemented it at the steak-house, I didn't sell just one lobster tail in the course of a year. In two and a half months, I sold *fifty*, and then went on to become one of the top door-to-door salesmen for a company that recruited me at that very restaurant. "What were the five words?" you are probably asking. Keep reading.

Most people agree that, in order to increase one's results and make a difference in as many lives as possible, it is important to increase the number of people that say "yes" to one's products or services. This can be a delicate subject for some. Most of us have either experienced or know someone who has experienced being taken advantage of by a person who cared more about getting richer than they did about serving the individual. That is not what this chapter is about.

There is a major difference between persuasion and manipula-tion. Manipulation creates a win-lose situation, and is done primarily for one person's gain over another. Persuasion creates a win-win situation, and is about helping a person overcome the mental and emotional blocks that have kept them from making decisions that will benefit them and their loved ones.

Recall what happened when you did the exercise during the rela-tionships chapter of greeting your friends and family members in dif-ferent ways and paying attention to how you felt during each one. Persuasion begins during the first ten seconds of meeting someone. People will determine if they like you or dislike you and if they will listen to what you have to say within only seconds of meeting you for the first time. This is why it is so important to focus solely on loving and benefiting people that you meet, especially if you hope to persuade them to listen to your message and join your cause. Remember to send them compliments in your mind; this will help to build *rapport.*

Rapport is the level of responsiveness between people. Building rapport means getting people to like and trust you and what you do. If they don't like or trust you, there is a pretty slim chance that they will want to do business with you. People tend to like others who are like themselves or are like those whom they want to become. One way to build rapport is to pay attention to and try to match the mannerisms of the person or people you meet. For example, pay attention to how fast they speak. If they are a fast talker, talk a little faster than you usually do to match their pace. If they speak very slowly, do the same. If they make certain expressions with their face or hands, find appropriate ways to do the same. Don't make it obvious that you are doing this or they may feel as if they are being mocked.

Proper rapport is one of eight major reasons why people say yes when presented with a product or service. The other seven include reciprocity, social proof, commitment, authority, scarcity, reason, and being asked.

Reciprocity

Have you ever gone to the grocery store when they had free samples of a new product out for you to taste and, after trying one, you felt more obliged to purchase it? This is a classic case of *reciprocity*, or feeling the need to give back after someone has given you something. We see this in many different forms in our society, the most common of which is feeling obligated to return a compliment when someone gives one to us. There are many ways to use this principle in your own business. If you have potential clients meet with you in your office, offering them a bottle of water when they sit down is a great way to utilize this principle. Gifting free samples of your product can be another effective method.

Social Proof

How many times have you been to a hotel and seen a little sign in the bathroom saying something to the effect of "Most people who stay in this room reuse their towels during their stay. Please help us conserve water." People tend to want to be included in the majority, so when they find out that the majority of people do a certain thing a certain way, they are more likely to follow suit. Studies have even shown that, when faced with a choice between two restaurants, most people will go to the one that is more crowded. If you offer products or services, make sure to have testimonials of others who will recommend your products or services. When people hear that others have had success with what you offer, they are much more likely to try it.

Commitment

Everyone has a different level of integrity, especially when it comes to keeping commitments, but studies have shown that people follow through with what they say they are going to do much more often if they have made a firm commitment to others. This is why I have my mentoring students make firm commitments to themselves and their family members to reach their goals, and I then follow up and hold them to their commitments. This is one of the reasons why my mentoring students have the success that they do; they have made solemn commitments and are then held accountable.

Authority

When I first began offering my services as a B.E.S.T. practitioner, it was extremely difficult for me to get people to pay me for treatments. They might try a treatment if I offered it to them for free, but, try as hard as I could, I just couldn't seem to build a clientele of paying patients. I soon realized that, because I was giving treatments at my house (which, at the time, was quite small), no one saw me as an authority figure. They had no problem paying to see medical doctors or chiropractors, but because I had no other title than my B.E.S.T. certification, they simply didn't value what I offered. Once I had space within a chiropractic office and dressed professionally, I was seen as a holistic healthcare provider and built a paying clientele quite quickly.

Find ways to add authority to what you do. You might consider renting a nice office space. You might want to associate with well-known names. You could even have loved ones write nice things about you and what you do to couple the authority principle with the social proof principle.

Scarcity

In 2012, Hostess Brands, famous for its cream-filled cupcakes, Ding Dongs, and Twinkies, announced that it would be going out of business after 82 years. This sent a wave of panic through the ranks of millions of Hostess fans, and people began to buy boxes and boxes of the goodies, knowing that the local store would soon be out of stock. Some of these products began to appear on eBay, with some selling for thousands of dollars when they would normally sell for a few dollars at most. Once their products became scarce, seemingly everyone wanted Hostess Brand treats.

I utilize this principle by rewarding clients who take action right away and sign up for products or services without delay. At my seminars, I generally offer free bonuses, such as audio training CDs, for the first so many people who sign up for additional classes and services. Because of the limited free bonuses as well as the limited seating available for my classes, people are more likely to take action when they feel impressed to do so rather than waiting around until the opportunity is lost.

Reason

A study at a major university indicated that the word "because" can actually have a significant impact on whether a person says yes or no. In this university's library, there is only one photocopy machine available for students to use, which can get quite busy at certain times of the day and lead to long lines. Those conducting the study would approach the person at the front of the line and ask if they could cut in front and use the photocopier before them, to which the answer was, as you can imagine, usually no. Then they tried a different tactic and added the word "because" followed by a reason and saw dramatically different results. They found that, if they gave a reason for wanting to cut ahead of everyone else, even if it was as silly as "Pardon me, I need to cut in front of you because I need to use the photocopy machine. May I?" the answer was yes more than 90 percent of the time.

Asking

Possibly the main reason people don't get what they want is that they don't *ask* for what they want. How many times have you fallen into this category? Perhaps you really wanted a date with a particular someone but didn't have the courage to ask that person out. Maybe you've really wanted a raise but never wanted to bother asking your supervisor for one.

When I worked in the restaurant industry, I would jokingly ask my managers, "Wanna buy me dinner tonight?" on a regular basis. I knew that the answer would probably be a no, but why not at least ask once in a while? To my surprise, they would occasionally say yes. If you never ask, the answer is definitely going to be no.

Life usually doesn't just hand us things. We have to ask and then take massive action in order to get them.

"But Eric, people are just so scary! What if they reject me and what I do?"

This is a major concern for many people. The fear of rejection has stopped countless individuals from going after their goals. How does rejection affect what you do?

Grab your success journal right now and answer the following questions: People are all . . .

I fear rejection because . . . I don't have everything that I desire in life because I have been unwilling to ask for . . . I commit to changing this in my life by . . . The results I will achieve by doing so are . . .

Once you've done this, read your answers to yourself out loud, place your hand over your heart, and say, "I'm awesome!"

Now that you understand some of the reasons why people say yes, we can discuss the major reasons why people say no and how to get past them.

Have you ever been approached by someone and, almost instantly, you knew that they were trying to sell you something? How did it make you feel? What triggered that feeling?

Every adult in this country has what's called a "salesman alarm" in their minds. We have been programed from a very young age to say no to salespeople because "all they want is your money." Certain phrases trigger this alarm and can actually cause people to reject you before you even have a chance to explain what you are offering. Let me give you an example.

Let's say you are walking down the road and a person that you have never met before approaches and asks, "Excuse me. Would you be interested in receiving a million dollars right now?" What would go through your mind? How would you respond? More than 75 percent of Americans say that they would be extremely skeptical if approached in this manner and would turn down the offer because they would feel like they are being sold to.

The phrase "would you be interested in . . ." is one that nearly always triggers the salesman alarm. Even if the offer was completely legitimate and the person who approached you was literally about to give you a million dollars in cash with no strings attached, you probably would have said no because of the approach.

Now let's try a different question. How would you respond if you were asked, "Would it be OK if you received a million dollars?" The overwhelming majority say "Yes!" What made the difference? It was the exact same question, so why do most people say no to the first one and yes to the second?

The words "would it be OK if . . ." are actually the five words that Tom Schreiter promised would change our lives, and boy, did they ever! This is a phrase that does *not* trigger the salesman alarm in others' minds. These are the words that I used to sell fifty lobster tails in just two and a half months while working at the Brazilian steakhouse. After taking each party's beverage orders, I would then ask, "Would it be OK if I shared some secrets to getting the most out of your experience here?" to which most people would reply yes. "Thank you. In addition to our regular meats that you can enjoy here tonight, there are a few items that can be purchased for an additional charge that really enhance your meal. We offer delicious grilled shrimp as well as incredible ten-ounce lobster tails that are gently steamed, served with drawn butter and fresh lemon wedges, and are absolutely to die for. They really help to make the meal better. Would it be OK if you enjoyed one?" While it's true that not everyone said yes, fifty people in two and a half months did, which is more than any other server had ever experienced.

Kids innately know this. You would never hear a child ask, "Mommy, would you be interested in letting me play outside?" They are very good at saying, "Mommy, would it be OK if I played outside?" Try this in your own life. Experiment with your friends and family. Replace "would you be interested in" with "would it be OK if" and see how many more people say yes.

Let's practice. Grab your success journal and write down several ways that you can use these five words. Then put your hand over your heart and say, "I'm awesome!"

Being Broke Sucks, So Stop It!

CHAPTER 8:

GOING AFTER YOUR DREAMS

Back in 1961, President John F. Kennedy announced to a worldwide audience that he wanted to put a man on the moon by the end of that decade. Do you think the rest of the world cheered and supported him on his goal? Not exactly. At the time, putting a man on the moon was such a preposterous idea that most of the world laughed at him. It was only eight years later in 1969 when Apollo 11 landed the first manned crew on the moon, proving the rest of the world wrong. This is the type of goal that Dr. Patrick Gentempo calls a "moonshot aim."

Grab your success journal and a pen. What is your moonshot aim? What is something that seems so far out there that the thought of even coming close to achieving it seems laughable? Is it to be a multimillionaire? Is it to live in a big, fancy mansion, complete with enough staff to keep it well cleaned and maintained? Is it simply to find a spouse or overcome an addiction? Write down your moonshot aim. At the top of the page, write "This is possible, and I get closer to it each and every day!" Now place your hand over your heart and say, "I'm awesome!"

The problem that stops most people is either (a) they don't have a moonshot aim, or (b) they simply don't believe it's possible for them, so they don't even try. I saw this a while back when I was attending a seminar put on by one of my mentors. The class was being held in downtown Salt Lake City, and across the street from the venue was a giant parking lot with enough space for hundreds, if not thousands, of cars. The parking lot was nearly full by the time I arrived the final day of the class. As I waited my turn to pay the parking fee and enter the lot, I watched as each car in front of me followed the car in front of it into the very back row of parking spaces, a good 5- to 10-minute walk away from the building where our class was being held. As I pulled my car forward, I thought to myself, "I wonder if there just happens to be a parking spot in the front row that no one else can see because they believe the only available spaces will be in the back." Rather than do what everyone else was doing, I drove my car to the very front of the lot, and sure enough, there was one empty parking space just waiting for me to pull in.

How many times have you done this? How many times have you had a goal and, because you didn't think it was possible, you simply did what everyone else did and figuratively pulled into the last row of parking spaces? Maybe you wanted to be rich but decided to do what everyone around you was doing and went to college, got good grades, got a degree, and got a job making $50,000 a year. Perhaps you've always wanted to lose weight, but because the rest of your family is overweight you've thought to yourself, "Why bother trying?" and continued along the unhealthy eating path that has led you to your current weight today.

Go after your dreams! Start believing in yourself! If you never even try, of course you'll never make it. You get exactly what you settle for and absolutely nothing more. If you settle for mediocrity, you'll be mediocre. If you decide to create success and happiness in all areas of your life, you will probably create success and happiness in all areas of your life.

Get out your success journal and answer the following prompts: I am not as successful as I would like to be because I have been unwilling to . . . I will do the following differently . . .

Then put your hand over your heart and say, "I'm awesome!"

Now that you recognize what your moonshot aim is and what you have been doing to stop yourself from achieving it, let's talk about how to go after it. If you are going to achieve it, you must learn how to *manifest* it into your life, beginning on the inside.

Think of a gorgeous fruit tree. The fruits came into existence because, years earlier, a seed was planted in the ground and roots began to take hold. After a certain period of time, the tree could be seen above ground and eventually bore fruit. The fruit is a result of the roots that are underground. If there are apple tree roots underground, the fruit above ground will be apples. If you have orange tree roots underground, you will end up with oranges. It's what lies underground that creates what is above ground. The roots create the fruit. The same is true in our lives.

Grab your success journal and write down the following formula:

Thoughts lead to emotions, emotions lead to actions, and actions lead to results.

It begins with our own roots, which we plant by way of our thoughts. Whatever we think about, we bring about. If we are constantly thinking negatively, negative results will show up in our lives. How many people do you know who seem to never stop complaining? Every time you're with them, all they do is whine about how crappy their lives are. Have you ever realized that the ones who complain the most seem to always have things to complain about? Have you noticed that those who tend to show the most gratitude in life seem to have everything going for them in life? Start by thinking about exactly what you desire and focus your thoughts on it until it brings a smile to your face.

Please be careful while doing this exercise. Make sure that you are not focusing on what you actually *don't* want rather than what you *do* want. For example, you might be thinking, "I want to be debt-free! I want to be debt-free!" The problem is that all your brain hears is the word "debt." Have you ever noticed that those whose sole focus is paying off debt seem to always have debt to pay off? It's because their biggest focus was "paying off debt," so circumstances always came into their lives to create debt to pay off. Try focusing on what you *do* want instead, like "I want to be financially free and abundant!" As you focus on these thoughts, create vibrant images in your mind and hold on to them until you begin to *feel* what it is like to have or experience whatever you are thinking about. These *feelings* will create *emotions*, such as happiness, joy, and bliss, which will ultimately lead you to taking *action.* Proper action can and will turn into *results*.

Combating Negativity

I joined the Boy Scouts of America through my church when I turned twelve years old and soon found out about an overnight camping trip my troop was planning to take. I had gone camping with my family before, but nothing matched my excitement about my very first overnight scouting experience. When the day of the trip arrived, I rushed home from school, packed my overnight bag, grabbed my pillow and sleeping bag, and started to head out the door. Just as I was about to walk down the steps of my front porch, my stomach began to churn and grumble. Deciding to ignore it, I met the others at the designated meeting place and threw my things in our scoutmaster's vehicle. There were a few other guys who had turned twelve about the same time I did, and we began to high-five each other and express just how excited we were for this campout. We made it about 30 minutes down the road when the uneasiness in my stomach returned, this time with a vengeance. I had only enough time to scream, "Here it comes!!" and stick my head out the window and watch all the contents of my breakfast and lunch fly through the air. It was only then that I realized there was a bus full of people just behind us. I still hope to this day that at least most of them had their windows up. The person sitting in the back seat of the car I was in had his window all the way down and screamed as chunks of cheeseburger landed on his face and clothes.

As you practice focusing on the things you desire, people may puke on you. Have you ever told a friend or family member that you wanted to achieve something huge, only to have them laugh in your face and tell you that you couldn't do it? This will certainly happen inside your mind, especially as you go for bigger and bigger goals. How many times have you thought about a goal and heard the words, "You can't do that! That's impossible! That will *never* happen to you!" inside your head? When this happens, celebrate! You are on the right track! When this happens, grab a piece of paper and begin writing these doubts and fears down to get them out of your mind. "But Eric, won't writing them down only reinforce them?" Not unless you go back and reread them. What you are doing during this exercise is transferring those limiting beliefs from your mind to paper, thus freeing up brain space to receive *action steps*. Action steps are ideas that are given to you in your mind which, if you write them down and do them, will ultimately lead you to achieving whatever it is you want to achieve. Action steps may not always make sense, and that's OK. The path to results is often highly illogical.

I learned this in a major way in 2014. I started the year on welfare, making less than $1,000 a month with my business. Thanks in part to working with the incredible mentors that I did, my income went up nearly every month, starting in January. August 2014 was the very first month I made $10,000 in a single month thanks to a check I received from my very first mentoring student on the last day of the month. I couldn't believe I had finally reached that milestone. I felt like I was on top of the world. It was only a few days later as I was focusing on my goals that the action step came to me to move into a bigger house. I thought I was going crazy. "Move into a bigger house now?" I thought. "I've only had one five-figure month so far. What if it was just a fluke and I never make that kind of money again? Shouldn't I wait until I see a track record before making that kind of leap?" The idea just kept coming to my mind: move into a new house as soon as possible. I could ignore it no longer.

I started looking at nice houses in the area, and took a Saturday to walk through two houses I had found listed online. One of them was a beautiful 3,700-square-foot home right between my two offices. It looked absolutely stunning, especially compared to the home I was living in, which was tiny, approximately 900 square feet. Within about a minute of entering the new home, I had a very clear feeling in my heart that said, "No, this house is too small for you."

I couldn't believe what I was hearing. How could a house that was more than four times the size of mine be too small?

The second house I looked at was more than 5,400 square feet and worth over $1 million. Located about ten minutes into Emigration Canyon, Utah, the home was beautiful and its surroundings were breathtaking. The moment I walked inside, I could tell that the home was extremely well taken care of and consisted of the finest of everything. Again, I had a very clear feeling about this home within a couple of minutes of entering, this time nudging me to move in. I nearly fainted. I looked at the numbers and didn't have any idea how I could possibly pull it off unless my business continued to grow and generate the five-figure-per-month income I had experienced only once before. It simply made zero sense to move into the home without a steady track record of success, but I couldn't deny my heart. So I signed the paperwork and moved my family in only a few short weeks later, still not knowing how I was going to duplicate the success I had experienced in August enough times to afford the house. Within a few days of exploring the home and getting settled, I realized I had a beautiful office where I could create and offer personal mentoring programs to my clients, starting at $15,000 each. Within four weeks of moving in, I had five people sign up for those programs, paying for the home for over a year. Every month since then, more and more people have signed up for personal mentoring programs with me, making it quite easy to afford the house. Though I had no idea when the action step first came to me, moving into a beautiful new home was actually an investment, one that generated a return on investment over and over and over again.

When those action steps come to you, write them down and then do them immediately. The biggest difference between the successful and the unsuccessful is that the successful take massive action when prompted to do so, while the unsuccessful don't. Failing to act when prompted to do so is a great way to show your brain that you don't actually want the goals that you have focused on. It may seem scary or illogical, but your heart will never lead you astray. Follow your heart and allow it to lead you to success.

Let's review one more time. Your thoughts lead to emotions, emotions lead to actions, and actions lead to results. With this in mind, are there things that you can do to help speed up this process?

One of the greatest tools that I have ever learned came from a former mentor of mine. He taught me the following process of how to use a *vision board* to train my brain to focus on the things, skills, and experiences that I desired and then to figure out how to achieve them. It was largely due to using a vision board that I was able to create a six-figure income my very first full calendar year in business and then do over $1.2 million in sales in only my second year in business. Designate a spot on the wall about eye level and near your bed so that you can see it as you are waking up for the day and as you are falling asleep at night. It doesn't have to be fancy. Don't try to be perfect with this. The longer you spend trying to make your vision board perfect without getting it on the wall, the longer you go without creating results. Choose a poster board or designate about a two feet by two feet space on your wall with some painter's tape or something similar. Then proceed to put images and statements of things that you want to achieve in that space, creating three rows and three columns of images and statements. Have no more than nine items, or goals, on your board; any more than nine and the brain becomes overwhelmed and isn't able to focus. Each morning, stand directly in front of your vision board and spend a few minutes looking at it. Take a moment to look intently at each goal during this time and tell your brain to get to work making it happen. As you do this exercise, have some paper and something to write with to remove the doubts that come to you, as well as to write out new action steps. Repeat this process at night before you go to sleep.

It is a good idea to have a variety of different goals, both short-term and long-term, on your vision board. The main purpose of the short-term goals is to boost your confidence by building evidence that you have the power to create. Put a few goals on there that will only take you a few hours or a few days to reach. Once you achieve them, celebrate your success. Create a special album on your social media page specifically for vision board success. Each time you achieve one of the goals, pull the image off the board, take a picture of the image, take a picture of you accomplishing whatever it is, and then post those pictures in this album. Not only will this help to prove to your mind that you are capable of manifesting amazing things into your life, it will also help to inspire others to reach their full potential. And yes, every time you pull an item off your vision board, replace it with a new goal. Once you've pulled a few smaller items off your vision board, your brain can work its way up to creating the larger items. The larger the item, the longer it may take to create it. Be patient with yourself. Know that this process of manifestation works, and a vision board is one of the fastest ways to speed it up.

Go right now, put some painter's tape or a poster board on the wall, and start taping images and statements onto it. Then put your hand over your heart and say, "I'm awesome!"

Sometimes things that you put on your vision board show up in unexpected ways. In early 2014, I put an image on my vision board that represented a special trip I wanted to take my wife on for our upcoming wedding anniversary. We had spent our honeymoon years earlier going amusement park hopping in Southern California, and I wanted to re-create our honeymoon, only this time in a much more lavish way. I estimated the trip would cost about $5,000 which, at the time, was a lot of money for me. I didn't have an extra $5,000 sitting in my bank account and had no idea how that money was going to show up. As I focused on this particular image one day, the idea popped into my mind to look up videos that people had posted online from their experiences in these different amusement parks. Many of these videos were made while people were on the actual rides, and as I watched them, I felt like I was actually there on the rides with them. The more videos I watched, the more I felt like I was there. This created something very powerful within me: a *belief*. A *belief* is a thought plus an emotion. I was allowing myself to get to the point that I would achieve this goal because, in my mind, I already had. I felt like I was there.

I did this exercise that I call *advanced visualization* during all my spare time for a week straight. That weekend, I received a text message from a client of mine who expressed the need to meet with me right away. Sensing the urgency, I invited her to meet me at one of my clinics. She proceeded to tell me that she had suddenly felt strongly prompted to sign up for a coaching program that I had just barely put together that would allow her to not only learn B.E.S.T. but also how to build a practice, increase her income, improve her health and relationships, and ultimately give her the opportunity to be hired as a full-time practitioner. She made a down payment and then wrote me a post-dated check to be deposited a few weeks later, which totaled $5,000. I was stunned. Did I really create the exact amount of money that I needed to fund this amazing trip simply by training my brain and then following the action step to meet with her when the opportunity presented itself? If this had only happened once, I could say that it was a coincidence, but these same miraculous events have happened time and time again since then.

Now that you have a vision board on the wall, choose one of the goals you want to focus on the most. Go online and find videos that represent this goal. For example, if your goal is to get a big, beautiful house, find and watch videos of people doing walk-throughs in big, beautiful houses. If your goal is to lose weight, find and watch videos that show other people's weight-loss transformations. Clear out the negative chatter in your mind and then follow the calls to action that come to you.

What do you do if it seems like action steps just aren't coming to you? This is an issue that many of my students have experienced. They hear me talking about following inspiration all the time, but they don't know how to receive it. If you are in the same boat, know that you certainly aren't alone. It simply means that something needs to happen to clear the channel of communication between you and your Higher Power.

Have you ever gone to bed but couldn't fall asleep because your mind was racing too fast? Do you constantly have a thousand things on your mind at any given moment? If this is the case, it could mean that your mind is too full to receive any more information. Think of your mind as being like a smartphone. I have a camera on my phone that I use regularly. If I have too many other things on my phone, including voice recordings, text messages, and pictures, my camera is unable to take more pictures because of the lack of data space. It isn't until I delete some of the existing pictures, text messages, etc., that I can then take more pictures. The same holds true with our minds. If you feel like you aren't receiving action steps, try clearing your mind. Start by making a *procrastination list*. Just as the name implies, this is a list of everything that you have been procrastinating. Once this is done, start going through the list and accomplishing what you have written down.

Any time you can't sleep, grab a journal and just start writing whatever comes to your mind. Inspiration often comes in the middle of the night when things are peaceful and distractions are few. There have been many times that I have woken up at 4 or 5 a.m. and not been able to go back to sleep until I wrote down everything that was on my mind. Some of my best ideas have come at this time. I also make sure to write down to-do lists for the following day as I am getting ready for bed. While most people spend their time filling their heads, I spend most of my time emptying mine.

My phone is another great resource for this. Any time a new idea comes to me, I instantly email it to myself. When the time comes for me to recall the thought and turn the idea into action, I can access the email practically anywhere.

Go get your success journal and create your procrastination list right now. Then put your hand over your heart and say, "I'm awesome!"

Meditation is another great way to clear your mind. Each night as I fall asleep, I listen to one of my favorite meditation tracks. There is soft music in the background and a guided relaxation that helps me to fall asleep quickly. As I drift into unconsciousness, the soft voice gives my mind positive suggestions that help me to increase my results when I am awake. Find a meditation track online that works for you and listen to it as you fall asleep.

Once you've done all of these, if you still feel you aren't getting clear answers, it could mean that there is something in your life that needs to be cleaned up. Look deep inside yourself. What could it be? Is there something in your past that you never made right? Is there a habit or addiction that prevents you from receiving answers? If you have religious leaders who help you overcome such things, speak to them. Allow them to assist you. Be completely honest and accept help when necessary. You can't be successful without inspiration, and inspiration can only come when you are ready, open, willing to receive it, and then willing to act. If you aren't willing to act, that inspiration will go to someone else who is.

You can do it, my friend.

CHAPTER 9:

SYNCHRONIZED!

I drove for thirty straight hours for my first experience with B.E.S.T. Little did I know that by doing so, I would be starting down a path that would change the course of my life forever.

It was the summer of 2011, and my wife and I were in Memphis, Tennessee, where I had landed a job selling alarm systems door-to-door. I was doing remarkably well; after only two weeks on the job, I was the top first-year sales representative in the region. While we were there, my wife received word from her parents about a three-day seminar that would be taking place in Provo, Utah, called Living Your Dream, taught by Dr. Roland Phillips, a world-renowned chiropractor and B.E.S.T practitioner. This called to us, as if heaven itself was giving us a sign that we needed to leave my job in Tennessee, make the long drive to Provo, and register for this seminar. At least that is what my wife tried to tell me. I was hesitant, but I couldn't shake the feeling that, even though I had no prior knowledge of the content of the seminar or what I could expect from being there, there was something very valuable that I would gain by being in attendance. Thank goodness I listened! Without informing anyone else of our decision to leave, we packed up our car, checked out of the hotel where we were staying, and made the thirty-hour trek west to Utah.

The first day of the seminar finally arrived, and I was as excited as I had ever been to start learning the secrets that I needed to start living my dream. I listened in awe as Dr. Phillips spoke of his experiences with the *Law of Attraction*, the power of positive thinking, and the use of vision boards. He explained that our emotions are a major factor in our feeling held back when it comes to going after our goals, and then used B.E.S.T. to clear those emotions out of us. This is something I had never heard of before. "How could my emotions affect my income? How could something that happened in the past affect the amount of success that I have now?" It all had to do with what had been lodged in my subconscious.

Think about it. Remember the example used before of being a young entrepreneur with a desire to become a millionaire. You go out and start a business, work extremely hard, put in ridiculously long hours doing everything you know to do to make your business successful, and it totally flops. You have to declare bankruptcy. On the other hand, you know some uneducated ding-dong who starts a business without any experience, and within a very short time he becomes massively successful. What happened there? What most people don't realize is that success all comes down to what the subconscious is programmed to create of it. For example, let's say you grew up in a home where you were taught that money is the root of all evil. What will you do with money, without even realizing it, when you get older? Probably push it away because, subconsciously, you believe that having money will cause you to be evil. This can be extremely frustrating for people who want to increase their results and become more successful, because their roadblocks aren't tangible or visible. Thankfully, Dr. Phillips presented a solution: the Bio-Energetic Synchronization Technique.

B.E.S.T. practitioners use various forms of muscle testing to check the subconscious for emotional and energetic roadblocks. Once a roadblock is found, a simple yet effective procedure is used to remove it. This allows the patient to heal physically, mentally, emotionally, and even financially. How different would your life be if you knew that nothing could hold you back from making all of your dreams come true? That is what B.E.S.T. does. It rids the body and mind of all those stoppers that keep you from living the life you truly desire.

As I sat there in that seminar, I remember feeling empowered and inspired, but also extremely confused. This whole concept was very new to me and, to be honest, I thought it was a bunch of hocus-pocus. How could simply "shifting my energy" and "clearing out emotions" that I could neither see nor touch make me wealthy and successful? While I thoroughly enjoyed the seminar while I was there, after returning home I began to resent the decision that my wife and I had made to spend the money to register. To make matters worse, my wife wanted to attend again a few months later and spend even more money!

Thankfully, as time passed, I began to research the concept of this form of healing and learned that it has a very real science behind it. I learned that B.E.S.T. was first developed by Dr. M. T. Morter Jr., a world-renowned chiropractor and holistic healthcare physician. What was ironic was that, even though Dr. Morter had practiced chiropractic therapy for decades and all his children were chiropractors, he suffered from back pain for decades. Figure that one out! Then one day, he attended a continuing education training where he was selected to be the guinea pig during a technique demonstration. He lay down on the table in front of everyone, thinking, "Thank heavens I was selected! This doctor will adjust me and get rid of some of this pain that I have." Unfortunately for Dr. Morter, that isn't how it panned out. The chiropractor giving the presentation simply addressed the audience and explained what he *would* do in theory given certain circumstances, while poor Dr. Morter was lying on the table thinking,

"Come on, cut to the chase! Adjust me already and help me get rid of some of this back pain!"

The presenter never actually did an adjustment, but Dr. Morter felt marvelous when he stood up. One of the other doctors made the connection that his body had actually adjusted itself which, from a chiropractic standpoint, should be impossible. He was stunned. How could this have happened? Having the brilliant scientific mind that he did, he set out on a quest to learn everything about the body that he could and, while doing so, developed the Bio-Energetic Synchronization Technique. He found that this technique was far superior to any other modality that he had learned or utilized in the past for two reasons:

1) He wanted to have a nonforceful way to adjust his patients. He realized that any time he would use the traditional chiropractic method of cracking, popping, and forcing the spine back into place, the patient's body would go into defense mode. This means that our bodies are extremely stubborn, and any time we try to force anything into place, the body will fight against that force. This is why you may have experienced receiving a traditional chiropractic adjustment only to feel your spine go right back out of place within a few hours or days. B.E.S.T. is very gentle. Zero force is used, allowing the body to hold the adjustment much more effectively.

2) The idea behind traditional chiropractic therapy back then was that misalignment of the spine was the cause of back pain, neck pain, shoulder pain, and so on. But what was causing the spine to be misaligned in the first place? You've probably heard the phrase "the body heals itself," which is very true. If we cut our finger, we don't have to consciously will the cut to heal; it simply does so on its own. So if something has caused the spine to become misaligned, what is keeping it that way? What is preventing the body from correcting and healing that problem? This is precisely what Dr. Morter wanted

to figure out. In his years of research, he learned that, in about 90 percent of cases, what was actually causing the spine to become or stay misaligned had to do with emotions and stress.

What happens is that our bodies hold on to stress from a number of different sources, including present, everyday stressors, concern for the future, even past events that we haven't been able to let go of, and these stressors will keep our bodies from healing. Once the stressors are removed, the body can heal itself. Once the *cause* is addressed, the *symptoms* naturally go away.

Imagine, if you will, that you are driving your car when the light on your dashboard turns on to tell you the car needs its oil changed. You pull into the nearest place that does oil changes, pay them for their services, and when you get your car back, you realize that, rather than changing the oil and fixing the problem, all they did was cover up the dashboard light so that you could no longer see it. Would you be a satisfied customer in that situation? Probably not. That's exactly what most people do when they have some sort of problem. What do they do if they have some sort of ache or pain? They pop a pill to no longer feel it. What do they do if their finances aren't going as well as they would like? They get a second job. What if they feel overly stressed or depressed? They take an antidepressant. This is what I call *covering up a symptom*.

Now let's say that, rather than simply covering your dashboard light, the mechanic popped open your front hood and cut the wire that was connected to your dashboard light, turning it off permanently, saying, "See? I found the cause of your issue. This was the wire that was lighting up your dashboard, and I took care of it for you. You're welcome." How satisfied would you be in this situation? This is what I call *treating* a symptom. It's a level above simply covering it up, but not by much. There are many wonderful modalities out there, including traditional chiropractic therapy, massage therapy, acupuncture, physical therapy, and the like. These modalities can all offer amazing temporary relief to a symptom and are much better than simply doing something to cover it up. The only problem is, in many cases, the relief is just that—temporary—because again, you are treating a symptom and not the cause.

Most people who hear this silly analogy look at me and say, "Of course I wouldn't just treat my dashboard if the light came on. That would be foolish. I would change the oil or find the cause of the problem." This is what differentiates B.E.S.T. from all other healing modalities. It finds and addresses the cause of the problem; therefore the symptoms naturally go away and stay away.

Everything that was said and done during that first three-day seminar was good and true. I simply needed time to find that out for myself. Over the course of the next four years, I intensely studied the Bio-Energetic Synchronization Technique as a holistic approach to helping someone heal, eventually certifying as a master practitioner and beginning a full-time practice of my own. I began to see miracles take place every day as more and more people felt the incredible power of B.E.S.T. in their lives.

This is why B.E.S.T. is such an effective tool when it comes to becoming wealthy; it locates and removes the negative programming from the subconscious and aligns, or synchronizes, your subconscious mind to your conscious goals and desires. It allows your brain to work for you instead of against you to create the life of your dreams.

You too can experience B.E.S.T. As a special thank you for reading this book, I would like to personally invite you and a guest of your choosing to meet with a Feel Well, Live Well B.E.S.T. practitioner (normally $100) free of charge. Simply use the contact information on the back cover of this book, let our office member know that you have read this book, and set up an appointment at your earliest convenience.

CHAPTER 10:

CHAMPION TRAINING

Georges St-Pierre is one of the most decorated mixed martial artists of his generation. He started training in Kyokushin karate at the young age of seven and soon entered the realm of wrestling, boxing, and Brazilian Jiu-Jitsu. After becoming a professional fighter at the age of 21, St-Pierre went on to become the welterweight champion of the world three times. When asked his secret to success inside the ring, he simply responded, "If you want to be a champion, you need to train like one."

People often ask, "How can I become successful more quickly? What can I do to set myself apart from the rest?" There are many qualities that make a person successful, but it primarily starts with what takes place inside a person's head.

We have already learned that there are two parts to the brain: the conscious and the subconscious, with the latter running the show. I understand the concept of training like a champion to produce champion results. Each day I perform a number of *mental* exercises to get my brain to continue to produce better and better results.

My day begins when my alarm goes off, and I intentionally hit the snooze button. I turn on a recording of myself sharing what my ideal life looks like in the present tense as if it has already come true. Because my mind can hear my own voice without my lips moving, it believes it to be my "inner voice" and instantly accepts it as truth. My alarm will sound again, and I will read a chapter in my scriptures. I then roll out of bed and onto my knees, where I express gratitude to my Creator for all the blessings in my life and ask for opportunities to serve Him and His children.

After a brief shower, I turn on my favorite "epic" song and look intently at my vision board.

As I focus on each goal, I immediately remove any doubts or fears that come to my mind until I am 100 percent clear and in tune with what must be done to achieve it. I then move in front of my list of *affirmations* and *afformations*. An *affirmation* or *declaration* is a statement made out loud to direct energy into something that you desire. For example, one of the affirmations that I say each day as I do my champion training is "I help millions of people around the world to be happy, successful, and live the life of their dreams!" The more energy and passion I put into my declarations, the more they expand and the faster they happen. This is why, throughout this book, I have had you place your hand over your heart and say, "I'm awesome." This is a declaration. It puts positive energy into your being "awesome." In your success journal, create a list of five or six declarations that you would like to give energy to each day. Then place your hand over your heart and say, "I'm awesome!"

An *afformation* is a way to lodge your *affirmations* in your subconscious mind. Inside the brain is what is called the *reticular activating system*, or RAS, which acts as a filter between the conscious and subconscious. Remember that your subconscious runs the show, so you want to get as much positive information into your subconscious as you possibly can. *Repetition* and *intensity* are what get your declarations past your RAS and into your subconscious, which can then go to work making your declarations a reality.

But could there be a faster way?

It has been estimated that it takes an idea ten thousand times to get through the RAS and into the subconscious. Let me give you an example. Let's imagine that you are having one of the worst days of your life and you would like to turn your day around. You could repeat to yourself, "Today is a wonderful day. Today is a wonderful day," with great intensity, but it would take up to ten thousand times to get that information into your subconscious and thus help to turn your day around. That is, unless you put your declaration into a "why" question. Any time you ask yourself a question, such as "Why is today a wonderful day?," your RAS instantly allows it through and sends your subconscious on a mission to figure out why today is a wonderful day. I have used this technique to create *massive* growth in my life. When I first quit my job waiting tables, my income goal was simply to replace my old income with my new business. I asked myself every day, "Why do I make at least $2,000 every month with my business? Why do I make at least $2,000 every month with my business?" Because my subconscious immediately went to work looking for ways to make this a reality, it did not take long for me to start making $2,000 each month with my business. I then moved my goal up to $3,000 each month, then $5,000, then $10,000, and so on. I used *afformations* to send my brain on a quest for answers and then turn my *affirmations* into reality.

For each of the *affirmations* you have written in your success journal, create an *afformation* to go with it. For example, if one of your *affirmations* is "I am successful in all areas of my life!," your *afformation* would be "Why am I successful in all areas of my life?" Once these are all written down, post your list of affirmations and afformations on the wall next to your vision board. Then place your hand over your heart and say, "I'm awesome!" ("Why am I awesome?")

As you read your list out loud, place your hand over your heart to activate *whole-brain learning*. This takes place when you can *see* it, *hear* it, *say* it, and *feel* it. Reading your list out loud allows you to see, hear, and say your affirmations and afformations, and placing your hand over your heart allows you to feel the vibration of the energy you are giving off.

Next I move on to my Who I Truly Am poster, which is just to the right of my vision board. Create a Who I Truly Am poster when you can be totally alone, without any distractions or disturbances. Have your success journal handy and something to write with, and kneel down and ask your Higher Power how He sees you. (You will need to remove the page you use, so you could use a separate piece of paper.) Do this until you get an image in your mind, and then draw that image to the best of your ability in your journal. Once you have finished drawing, write down all of the characteristics of the image that you see. You could write "beautiful, intelligent, charismatic, wealthy," or whatever comes to you. At the top of the paper, write Who I Truly Am. If this is how your Higher Power sees you, this is who you truly are. Looking at the drawing of who I truly am and the characteristics I truly possess makes a huge differ-ence for me when I go about the day. If I feel tempted to make a bad decision, the image of my poster will pop into my mind and will remind me that such a decision isn't becoming of the man I truly am. Place your poster to the right of your vision board and, with your hand over your heart, read through the characteristics you have written. Get a good image in your mind of your true identity. You may be surprised how big a difference this will make for you. Your Who I Truly Am poster will be a powerful way to keep your personal value high.

Finally, I do an exercise called the *Morter March*, named after Dr. Morter, who developed B.E.S.T. I begin the exercise by doing a simple muscle test. Place the tips of your thumb and pointer fingers together on your nondominant hand—meaning if you are right-handed, you would place the tips of your thumb and pointer finger together on your left hand. Then place your right pointer finger through the hole you have just created with your left hand. Go ahead and try this right now. If you are left-handed, do the opposite. You are now going to have a contest between your two hands. With your right pointer finger, you are going to try to break through the two fingers on your left hand, and your fingers on your left hand are going to try to hold strong and keep your right pointer finger from breaking through. This may take some practice, but will not be too hard after time. Once you get it down, your left hand will usually win against your right finger, unless you think or say a negative thought. Go ahead and try the following: place your finger in the hole again and say "give me a yes" and try to break through your left two fingers. If you do this correctly, it should hold strong and your finger should not be able to break through. Then say "give me a no" and repeat the process. This time your right finger should be able to break through your left two fingers. This is how you do a muscle test and how you can actually find out if your subconscious is on board with your conscious desires. If it is, you can think about or look at an image of one of your goals, do this test, and it will stay strong. If it isn't, your left two fingers will be weaker, and you will be able to break through with your right finger. This is the goal that you will need to focus on when you do this next part of the exercise.

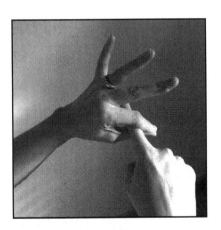 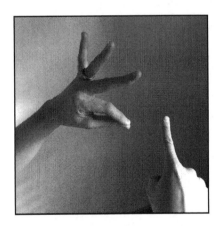

Go through the items on your vision board and do this muscle test until you find a goal that causes you to go weak. Now proceed with the next part of the *Morter March,* which is a special stretch that will put you in a position that you're not normally in. Doing this causes the mind to say, "Whoa, time out here. We weren't meant to be in this position. What is going on?" Distracting this part of the brain allows your subconscious to locate and remove roadblocks that are keeping

you from accomplishing whatever your goal happens to be. Start by putting your left foot forward and bending your left knee just enough so that you can no longer see your foot. Your right leg goes back and remains straight, with your feet parallel to each other. Now extend your right arm up in front of you at a 45 degree angle, and extend your fingers wide so that your right thumb is pointing up. Your left arm will go back at a 45 degree angle as if you were making a straight line from your right hand to your left hand, with your fingers extended and your left thumb pointing down. Now tilt your head slightly toward your extended left hand, close your left eye, look up at your extended hand with your open right eye, and hold your breath for ten seconds, closing both your eyes for the final two seconds. Now breathe out and change to the other side. You will now put your right foot forward, bending the knee. Raise your left arm in front of you, extend your fingers, thumb pointing up, and put your right arm back, fingers extended with your thumb pointing down. Tilt your head slightly toward your left arm, close your right eye, and hold your breath for 10 seconds, closing both eyes for the final two. Repeat this process three times on each side. You will look and feel so silly doing this the first time, but I promise there is a science behind it. If you still have trouble doing this after reading these instructions several times, simply look up the Morter March online. You can find photos and videos of people demonstrating how to do the exercise on the internet.

Once you feel confident performing this exercise, you can add afformations in your mind. Putting yourself in this weird position instantly creates an opening in your RAS, allowing you to feed positive ideas directly into your subconscious. If I am focusing on a particular goal—for example, having a vibrantly healthy body—I will ask myself in my mind, "Why do I have a vibrantly healthy body?" as I am in this position. I will ask myself the question twice with one eye open, then one more time once both eyes are closed. Then I take another breath, switch sides and do it again until I have done it three times on each side, having repeated the question "Why do I have a vibrantly healthy body," or whatever it is I am focusing on, a total of eighteen times.

Now I know what you must be thinking, and that's, "Oh my goodness, is that ever hokey!" Well, the way I look at it is that I'd rather be really hokey and really successful than really cool and really broke. How about you? I love what one of my mentors used to say: "It's only hokey if it doesn't work." And the Morter March works every time. Make the Morter March a part of your champion training. You'll be so glad you did.

This routine sets me up for success throughout the day. My mind is focused on my purpose, which allows me to be constantly seeking out ways to achieve it. My evening champion training includes many of my morning rituals, plus an entry in my *celebration journal.* A celebration journal is a notebook that you keep next to your bed and write in just before going to sleep. Each night, open it, date it, and then write at least one or two accomplishments from the day. These could be enormous accomplishments like getting married, reaching your ideal weight, or creating a million-dollar business, or they could be small accomplishments. "I am still breathing," or "I put on clean underwear this morning" are perfectly acceptable for this exercise.

Obviously, if you have more than one or two accomplishments to celebrate, do so. You are certainly not limited. To the subconscious, an accomplishment is an accomplishment. The more you write in your celebration journal, the more evidence you build of being *accomplished.* Remember, we attract more of whatever we celebrate, so I celebrate my daily wins so that I can receive many more of them.

Find a journal that you can use exclusively for celebrating your daily accomplishments, write "Celebration" on the front, and place it by your bed. Then place your hand over your heart and say, "I'm awesome!"

Once I have completed my daily entry in my celebration journal, I say another prayer of gratitude to my Creator and report accomplishing the things that He inspired me to do throughout the day. Finally, I fall asleep to a meditation track. I want my mind to be filled with positive affirmations as I go into unconsciousness. You can find plenty of meditation tracks online that are designed to help you with whatever goal you desire to achieve. For example, if your chief goal right now is to lose weight, look up Weight Loss Meditation and choose one that works for you. You are also welcome to purchase a copy of The Greatness Within You if you would like, which is an audio CD filled with both affirmations and afformations to help you in *all* areas of your life. Simply go to www.FeelWellLiveWell.com to get a copy.

Create these daily habits. Train like a champion and allow champion results to come into your life.

CHAPTER 11:

MINDSET OF MILLIONAIRES

Now that you are nearing the end of this book, go back and retake the questionnaire that you took in Chapter 2. Write your new answers inside your success journal and compare them to your original answers. Did any of them change? Now that you have greater insight into how rich and successful people think, let's take a closer look and review some of the principles illustrated in the questions.

Questions 1, 3, 6, and 13 all have to do with your relationship with your Higher Power and your ability to follow inspiration when it comes. Remember, the path to success is usually quite illogical. It usually isn't what your family members think it is or what your current group of friends think it might be. It didn't make any logical sense for us to move into our big home in 2014, but because we followed through with the inspiration that came to us, our results increased in a major way. Trust your heart. It will never lead you astray.

Questions 2, 5, and 8 have to do with being a "no matter what" type of person. Napoleon Hill says that unsuccessful people tend to be very slow to make up their minds and very quick to change them. They are the "I'll think about it" type of people. They hesitate when presented with decisions to make, hoping that the opportunity will present itself later or that their circumstances will somehow be different in the future. The thing about those people is that they typically don't end up taking the opportunities presented to them, and their lives and results generally stay pretty much right where they are. Napoleon Hill continues that, on the flip side, successful people tend to be very quick to make up their minds and very slow to change them. Once they are presented with an opportunity, they follow their hearts. If their hearts tell them to take action, they take action immediately. When? Immediately. They figure out a way to make it happen, even if that means leaving their comfort zones.

If you want to be successful, you must learn how to make decisions quickly. The best opportunities usually aren't around for very long. What's interesting is that questions 2 and 8 are nearly identical in nature, even if they don't appear to be. They both have to do with seeing an opportunity to receive a return on investment and finding a way to get whatever is needed done immediately.

My friend, if you are ever in a position similar to what question 2 describes and your heart tells you to take action immediately, do it! Borrow the money from a friend or charge it to a credit card if you have to, but take the opportunities that are right for you before they are no longer available.

Questions 4, 9, 11, 14, and 20 all have to do with how you view money and those who have it.

There are many people who justify being broke by saying that money isn't that important. T. Harv Eker says that anyone who says that money isn't that important probably doesn't have any. Can you imagine if you said that your husband or your wife wasn't that important? Do you think that they would be around very long? Of course not, and neither would money.

Money is neutral. It is simply a tool that can be used for good or evil, so let's be people who have lots of money and use it for good!

The same goes for borrowing money. Remember that there is a difference between *debt* and *loans.* How you use the borrowed money determines whether it becomes good debt or bad debt.

It's also important to view rich people as you would other people. If you believe that rich people are all dirtbags, are you going to want to become rich? Of course not! An old saying goes, "Bless that which you want." If you want to be rich, try looking up to and modeling other rich people. Even ask them to teach you how to achieve similar results.

Questions 10, 15, 18, and 19 all have to do with your ability and desire to keep moving forward. What differentiates most middle-class people and rich people isn't that rich people have goals and middle-class people don't. It's just that rich people tend to set their sights a little higher and want to get there as quickly as possible, while many less successful people don't mind taking the low and slow route because it's more comfortable.

The key word in that is, of course, comfortable. Middle-class people tend to be very hesitant when it comes to doing things that cause them to move outside their comfort zone. Rich people, on the other hand, understand that growth only takes place outside one's comfort zone. They constantly train their bodies and their minds through such things as exercise, meditation, reading, and daily champion training.

They also understand the importance of having a personal mentor who can help them make it through life's turbulent moments and get results faster by being another set of eyes that can see things from a different perspective. Think about Olympic athletes for a moment. You will never see an Olympic athlete without a coach. They are the best athletes in the world, usually even better than their trainers, but they realize that having that extra pair of eyes teaching them how to train could mean the difference between victory and defeat.

Middle-class people tend to try to learn everything themselves. You would be hard-pressed to get a middle-class person to invest in a personal mentor, but rich people understand the mantra that says, "He that is self-taught has a fool for a master." Why would a successful person take the low and slow route when a good mentor can save them time and help them reach their goals much faster? When their mentor tells them to do something, they go and do it. They know that their mentor has had success by doing certain things, so when they learn how to do the same thing, they go out and do it. It may not make sense, but they trust their mentors enough to follow their suggestions.

Never ever stop learning. Never stop growing. Read books by authors in your field. Listen to audio books, continue to further your education, and learn how to overcome your fears.

This brings us to question 12 about public speaking. It amazes me that public speaking is the number-one fear on the planet. Most people can't stand the idea of getting up in front of other people and delivering a message. This comes from a very debilitating way of thinking: perfectionism.

May I tell you a secret? As long as you are a human being living on this earth, you are going to be imperfect, and so will everyone else around you, including the richest and most successful people. What separates them from the rest is that they act in spite of their imperfections.

I make mistakes during every presentation I give and every seminar I teach, but I don't let it stop me from continuing to give presentations and teach seminars. I wasn't perfect when I first started my business, nor am I perfect now. I realized that I had to start somewhere and that perfection only comes by making mistakes and learning from them.

Question 17 has to do with your ability to deal with stress. There will be many stressful moments along your journey to success, and you must have a way to deal with stress in a healthy and positive way.

If you haven't listened to my CD titled Leaky Joy Tank, get a copy of it and listen to it. It contains some fantastic tools for eliminating stress. Make sure you have an exercise plan, take time out of your day to meditate for a few minutes, get good sleep at night, and find a good B.E.S.T. practitioner.

If you're reading this book and you have never experienced B.E.S.T., find a practitioner as soon as you can. Take advantage of the offer to see one of our practitioners at no charge by using the contact information on the back of this book. You'll be glad you did.

Question 7 deals with your ability to keep your commitments. How are you doing in this arena, my friend? Are you a person of your word? Or do you say you'll do things when you don't really intend to do them? If you want to become rich, people around you must feel that you are an honest person, a man or woman of integrity.

"Oh, but Eric, what about the rich people who lie and steal and manipulate others?"

Those people are very much the minority. And watch what usually happens to those people. Over time, karma eventually catches up to them. If people are going to invest in your products or services, you have to follow through on what you say you'll deliver. Yes, this starts with even the little things, like keeping a commitment to a friend, even when things are tough at home.

Finally, we come to question 21. What would your three wishes be? I'm going to uncover something that may rattle you a little bit, and that's the fact that these three wishes tend to reflect your greatest fears. For example, if you said, "I wish I had lots of money," there's a part of you, deep down, that probably fears either not having enough or losing money. If you wished for a better marriage, there's probably part of you that fears divorce. Take a look at what you wished for and try to figure out where those fears stem from. Once you figure it out, grab your success journal and start writing "I fear losing . . . because . . ." Write down whatever comes to you. Once you have done this for all three of your wishes, remove that piece of paper from your journal, crumple it up, and say, "Thank you for showing me what my fears were, but now you have no power over me, and I release you." Take that paper outside, put it in a metal bucket or grill, light it with a match, and watch it burn. You can do this exercise for all your fears. Write them down, journal on where these fears come from, then light that page with a match and burn it. Then place your hand over your heart and say, "I'm awesome!"

CHAPTER 12:

WEATHERING THE STORMS

If you are one of the many who, as you have read this book, have thought, "This is all fine and dandy, but this just isn't for me. Eric's life is too perfect, and mine is too hard. I'll never be able to live the life of my dreams," you are not alone. There are many who simply don't see what goes on behind the scenes in a successful person's life. They don't see all of the hard work, the discouragement, the fear, the doubts, the turbulence, or the judgment. All they see are the big houses, the fancy cars, and the luxurious vacations. This chapter is specifically designed to help you see that even the most successful people don't have everything figured out, as some may think. We have just as many problems, trials, and difficulties as anyone else. Our trials may be a little different from those of others, but life isn't perfect for us in any way, shape, or form. As you read this chapter, please keep an open mind and remember, if I can achieve success, so can you!

It was 1947 when Chuck Yeager of the US Air Force became the first man to break the sound barrier (about 767 mph). According to one person's account of the events, the US military was trying to find a way to be able to attack their enemies in such a way that they wouldn't be detected by radar. Many had attempted to break the sound barrier before, but none had succeeded because their airplanes would begin to shake so violently when their speed would approach the sound barrier that they were often ripped apart and destroyed. Naturally, very few people were willing to attempt the feat.

Chuck Yeager eventually stepped up and volunteered to test a new kind of airplane, one that was built to withstand incredibly high speeds. When the day came, he was hooked up to all of the equipment that he needed, including his two-way radio to communicate with those who were back at the base, and took off. Everything went smoothly until his speed began to approach the sound barrier, when, like so many other planes that had attempted this before, his plane began to shake violently, to the point where he nearly lost all control. Those who were back at base yelled through the radio for him to slow down, pull back, and come back, for it just wasn't worth the risk that he was going to undertake. They all believed at that moment that, if he went any faster, his plane would explode and Yeager would die.

How many times have you felt this way? How many times have you begun to make progress toward a certain goal, and everything goes just the way you want it to go . . . until the turbulence begins and it seems like everything falls apart? What did you do? Did you pull back your efforts and retreat into your comfort zone?

I can only imagine what must have gone through Yeager's mind as he felt his airplane begin to spiral seemingly out of control, not wanting to back down from his goal but not wanting to die either. As his plane continued to scream in protest and as his associates continued to yell into the radio for him to come back to base where it was safe, he did what few people would have had the courage to do: he punched his acceleration lever, causing an enormous *boom*. Everyone who was listening at the base thought that his plane had exploded and that Yeager was dead.

There was a silence for several moments, until finally Yeager's voice came over the radio, "Whoa . . . it is smooth sailing on the other side."

I cannot count how many times that, by simply withstanding the turbulence of life and getting through the difficult times, I have found myself staring at incredible rewards on the other side. The key is to simply weather the storm and stay with it.

The following is an anecdote from www.betterlifecoachingblog.com:

In his all-time classic book, *Think and Grow Rich*, Napoleon Hill tells the story of R. U. Darby.

Darby's uncle had gold fever, so he staked his claim and started digging. After a lot of hard work, the uncle found a vein of ore, so he covered up his find and returned home to raise the money for the machinery that he would need to bring the ore to the surface.

They raised the money and Darby traveled with his uncle back to the site to make their fortune.

Things started well, and before long, they had enough to clear their debts. They were excited; everything from here on would be profit, and things were looking good.

Then the supply of gold stopped. The vein of ore had disappeared.

They kept on digging, but found nothing.

After a while, they quit in frustration and sold their machinery to a junk man for a few hundred dollars.

After they went home in disappointment, the astute junk man called in a mining engineer, who checked the mine and calculated that there was a vein of gold just three feet from where Darby and his uncle had stopped digging.

The junk man went on to make millions from the mine.

Darby returned home, paid back everyone who had lent him money and was determined to learn from his mistake in giving up too soon.

I'm sure you've heard the story of the troops who, centuries ago, had only one chance to win the war, which was to sail to a particular island and fight until they took over the island. Once they arrived, their commander burned the ship so that the troops couldn't chicken out and try to retreat. They now only had two options: win the war by taking over the island or die.

When faced with choosing between success or death, people tend to succeed! My friend, if you desire success in your life, don't allow any other options. The marriages that succeed are the ones where divorce simply isn't an option. The men and women who beat cancer are the ones for whom death isn't an option! People tend to do the things that they must do and only some of the things that they should do. You *must* eat to stay alive. You *must* have water to stay alive. Make success a *must* and simply make it happen. Period.

Go right now and grab your success journal. Make a list of all the times you have stopped figuratively three feet from gold in your own life, and then compare this list to the one you made in Chapter 4 of all the reasons why you have ever failed. How different would your life be right now if you had continued to make progress toward your goals in the past rather than giving up when you did? Next to this list, write down your firm commitment to stick with your goals until you achieve success. Now place your hand over your heart and say, "I'm awesome."

You might be reading this and still be thinking, "Eric, that's great, but you just don't know my story! I'm different!"

The truth is you're absolutely right. I don't know what circumstances you were born into. I don't know how hard your life has been or your specific reasons for not being where you desire to be in life. The thing I do know is that your circumstances don't shape your destiny.

I know of many, many people who were born into the most loving of families, were taught correct principles, received the best education possible, and had all the resources imaginable, and yet spent most of their lives in and out of rehab. On the other hand, I know of many people who were born into unbelievably abusive homes, experienced every horror imaginable, and yet became some of the greatest and most successful people on this planet.

I once heard someone say, "It's not my fault if I'm born poor, but it is my fault if I die poor." It's time to get out of victim mode and take responsibility for your life. If there's something about your life that you don't like, change it. Period.

Easier said than done? Of course. But is it impossible? Absolutely not! Remember that those who say that they can and those who say that they can't are both usually right.

"Oh, but Eric, you just don't get it! My life isn't all rosy like yours is."

Ha! A major mistake that people make is thinking that the lives of successful people are perfect. I'm here to tell you that is not the case. All most people see is the big house, the nice cars, and the exotic vacations, so when they want to improve their lives and they go through some hard times, they throw their hands up in the air because they think they're doing something wrong and have no one to relate to.

Please allow me to tell you a little about my journey to where I am today. As I do so, I do not seek sympathy. In fact, you might be someone who reads this and thinks, "That's it? That's all he's gone through? I've gone through *much* worse!" I recognize that there are many people who have gone through much worse than I have. My purpose in getting very personal with you in this chapter is so that, hopefully, you can relate in some small way to something I say and have been through, and that a switch in your mind flips and you think, "Well, if he can do it, I can do it!"

I was conceived out of wedlock to a young woman who had an extramarital affair with one of her co-workers. Rather than aborting me, she put me up for adoption through my church's family services, something for which I will be forever grateful. I was placed in a foster home for the first three months of my life because of the time it took to find my biological father and get him to sign adoption papers.

I grew up in a home where contention abounded. My adoptive parents never seemed to be happy. My father was deeply entrenched in an addiction to pornography. He and my mother were constantly fighting and yelling at each other which, of course, translated into making our house an extremely stressful place in which to live. When I was a junior in high school, I took a test to see how high my levels of stress were. My score came back five times higher than what was deemed a dangerous level of stress for someone my age. It is a miracle that I didn't experience major health challenges during that time of my life.

As you have already read, my parents eventually divorced as I was about to turn 18. I always knew that this would eventually happen, but I wasn't prepared for the difficulty of the decision I had to make regarding which parent I was going to live with. After much thought and prayer, I decided to spend half of the time with my mother, who would be moving into the house that had belonged to my grand-mother, and half of the time with my father, who had informed me that he would be renting a two-bedroom apartment, starting Thanksgiving Day of 2004.

My mother always hosted Thanksgiving dinner at our house, and this year was no different. My plan was to enjoy the holiday meal with my family, pack my bags, and then head back to my dad's apartment to spend the night. As I was walking out the door toward his car, he asked me, "Where do you think you're going?" I responded that I was going to spend the night at his apartment just as we had previously discussed. "No you're not," was his reply. "I turned your bedroom into an office."

I came to find out that my father had turned what was going to be my bedroom into a sanctuary for his addiction and later into a bedroom for an 18-year-old girl that he introduced me to as one of his "models." Apparently he had gone as far as producing pornography, including with this teenage girl he was now living with. I was absolutely heartbroken. Because I hadn't chosen to live with him full-time, he had chosen to feed his addiction rather than our relationship. I felt rejected, worthless, and abandoned. It was several months before I heard from him again. He later told me that he no longer wanted to have me as a son because I was a "disgrace to the Bailey name" for wanting to follow my dreams and become successful. It has taken every ounce of mental and emotional strength to forgive him.

Years later, after serving as a missionary for my church, getting married, and graduating with a degree from Dixie State, I went on to study Spanish translation at Brigham Young University. It had been my dream for some time to become a full-time Spanish-to-English interpreter. My final year came, and I felt like I was in the wrong place, as if continuing to pursue this higher degree wasn't where I was supposed to be. I knew that if I simply dropped out of school, there would be some serious consequences to pay from my family, especially from those who had helped me financially to pursue my degree. Sure enough, when I announced my decision to leave BYU and study the Bio-Energetic Synchronization Technique through Morter Health System, I was called every name imaginable. This fear of judgment *almost* stopped me from pursuing my true calling in life, which was helping people heal and, eventually, mentoring.

After quitting my full-time job in 2013, it wasn't long before my family and I had to go on welfare. I had no business experience, and my income continued to drop lower and lower before we finally were able to turn things around. Reaching out for outside assistance was one of the most difficult things I had ever done. I simply couldn't believe that a person like myself, someone who had been told his entire life how talented he was, would have to humble himself to the point where he could allow someone else to provide the basic necessities for his family. Ironically, it was when I became totally OK with being on welfare that things started looking up for us. Once I began to be grateful for everything we *did* have rather than bitter about everything we *didn't* have, our situation began to improve. We learned that right before a new breakthrough took place, we always experienced a period of turbulence. Just like Chuck Yeager experienced the most difficult part of his flight right before he hit his goal, life tends to test us just before we make breakthroughs.

I was scheduled to teach a full-day relationships seminar in southern Utah in May of 2014. Several people had registered, including a couple who had been on the verge of divorce for many years and were desperate for anything that could help them pull things together. They would be traveling hundreds of miles to be at this seminar, and I didn't want to let them down.

That's when bronchitis hit.

The day before my wife and I were to make the trip to southern Utah, I sat down at my kitchen table feeling absolutely rotten. I was coughing harder and more often than I ever had in my life. "How could I possibly deliver a class like this?" I thought to myself. "There's no way I can deliver a 12-hour presentation if I can't even effectively speak an entire sentence without coughing." What made things worse was that, just two weeks earlier, I had taught a different full-day seminar in southern Utah that went absolutely horribly. If history was going to repeat itself, it just didn't seem worth it to try to make the trip a second time.

My wife saw my concern and sat down beside me. "I think I may have to postpone the class," I told her. She gently reminded me that I had made a commitment to those who would be attending, and that one couple in particular was depending on this class to hold their marriage together. While I couldn't see how things could possibly work out for us or why this seminar would be any different from the one two weeks earlier, I relented to keeping the class on the day it was originally set.

I am so grateful that I did.

This class was dramatically different from the last one. Everything went as smoothly as it could go, and the couple that made the long trip to be there was so grateful for the experience. Years later they are still together, happier and more in love than ever before.

Similar patterns happen in our lives each time we are about to reach a new level of success. How many times has this shown up in your life? Perhaps you were getting ready to go to a life-changing seminar and someone in your family got sick or your car broke down, making it much more difficult to go. Maybe a massive wave of panic struck you just before you were to give a presentation that would have launched your business. Nearly every time we are within a week of teaching one of our seminars or have a new audio CD coming out, my wife and I will have some of the worst disagreements of our marriage. Thankfully, we are now able to recognize those patterns of turbulence when they show up and quickly use the tools that we teach to clear ourselves and make things right. We know that if we allow turbulence to dictate our decision, we will lose the rewards that follow.

Grab your success journal right now and write about this subject. Identify patterns of turbulence in your own life that tend to show up just before a reward comes. Once you identify these patterns, you can recognize them when they happen in the future and quickly get through them. You may be surprised at the rewards that follow.

In Chapter 4, I mentioned investing $5,000 in a six-month course taught by a man that I highly admired. He was everything I wanted to be in life. He was the father figure I had always craved. Early in the six-month program, I had an opportunity to spend a few hours one-on-one with him, and it was one of the best experiences of my life. I wanted to be like this man in every way, so when I found out that he offered opportunities to mentor with him one-on-one for a year for $25,000, I immediately put it on my vision board.

Because of the information I learned during the six-month program, my income quintupled in only four months. I was absolutely shocked that such a feat was possible. But then it plateaued. For three months, I couldn't seem to raise my income any higher. I realized that, although I had experienced marvelous growth during the group trainings in the six-month program, I needed a personal mentor who could see what my personal blocks were and help me customize a plan of action for my growth. I called a woman who worked under the above-mentioned gentleman as a mentor and trainer and asked her what she could do for me. She gave me a price (which was not inexpensive), and I paid her in full.

Only five days later, I was driving to my office when a very powerful impression came over me. "Now that you've hired her, go hire him," meaning hire the man I had idolized to personally mentor me. I couldn't understand why I would be receiving that action step before I had even begun to mentor with the woman under him. I sent her a text message asking her what I should do, to which she replied that she would need to call me later that day. When she did, she got right to the point.

"Here's the thing, Eric. Just this morning he announced that he wasn't going to do personal mentoring anymore."

I was horrified! I had waited too long, and now I wouldn't be able to get the coaching I needed to reach the success I knew I was capable of. "But," she continued—and inside I thought to myself, "Thank heavens for buts!" "But, he knows who you are and has actually been wanting to work with you, so if you can get the funds in right away, he will make an exception and will go ahead and mentor you. How soon can you come up with the tuition?"

Have you ever had an experience where a word came out of your mouth that didn't actually come from you? As if your mouth had a mind of its own and spoke for you? That happened to me, because as soon as she asked me that question, the word popped out, "Tomorrow."

What?!?

Are you kidding me? How in the world was I supposed to come up with $25,000 in 24 hours?!? There's no way!

Once my shock and confusion finally wore off, I began to rack my brain for answers. "How am I to create $25,000 in 24 hours?" I repeated in my mind. The more I did this, the more ideas and action steps began to come to me. They didn't make too much sense, but I wrote them all down and completed every single one of them, until, 24 hours later, I called this same woman on the phone and expressed with great excitement, "I've got the $25,000. I'm in!"

I couldn't believe that this was actually happening! I now had the chance to mentor one-on-one with my idol, the man who meant everything to me and whom I wanted to be like. This enormous vision board item was finally coming off. It was about that time that my logical brain realized what I had done and began to put up a fight.

"Are you kidding me, Eric?" I heard in my mind. "You just spent $25,000! Are you crazy?" I freaked out for the next week or two, because spending that kind of money simply didn't make sense. Thankfully, I learned a long time ago to follow my heart rather than my brain, so I stuck with my decision and began to mentor one-on-one with these two amazing individuals.

It was better than I could have even imagined.

My business flourished and my income skyrocketed, so much so that my mentor asked me to participate in giving testimonials and mini trainings on his stage during several of his seminars. I was his poster child. He featured me in *Utah Business* Magazine and even had *Forbes* Magazine do an article about me.

Subconsciously, I had finally filled the void I had so desperately yearned for. My mentor was more than a father figure, more of a godlike figure to me. I had gained his approval, so that meant that I was good enough.

Then it all came crashing down.

Within the span of a few short months, multiple people who had done business with me decided to take some things that I had said the wrong way and began to slander my name. They went so far as to contact my mentor and explain how horrible I was, that I was a manipulator, a liar, a fraud, and every other disgusting name imaginable. They shamed my mentor for training me and said that they wanted nothing to do with him or his business because of his association with me. This began to escalate until one day, he asked me to meet him at his office. When I arrived, he told me of the situation and that his good reputation that he had worked so hard to build was being tarnished because of me. Therefore, he needed to cut ties with me. I was no longer his mentoring student, and I was no longer welcome at his events.

I was absolutely crushed. Here was the man that I had idolized for so long kicking me out of his program and telling me that he no longer approved of me or what I do. Again, to a degree, this man was a very godlike figure in my mind; therefore if he didn't approve of me, neither did God, so what reason did I have to continue to live?

I went home that evening, burst into tears, and prayed to my Father in Heaven to please take my life. I couldn't bear the burden of continuing to live if nothing I did was good enough.

I want to make it clear that I hold no bitterness toward my former mentor. Please do not judge or think ill of him for simply doing what he felt he needed to do to protect his business. We have communicated a number of times since that day and have, if nothing else, a cordial relationship.

Throughout all these difficulties I also battled with addiction. While I won't go into detail about that subject, let's just say it has caused me unbearable grief and has been something that I have spent many hours with my religious leaders to clear up.

I absolutely hated myself. Here I was, this professional mentor and trainer, experiencing things that most people only dream about, and yet I could not stand to look at myself in the mirror because of the shame and the heartache from all the mistakes that I had made and all the people I had hurt. This led me to turn to food, particularly sugar, to help numb the pain, and I put on a lot of weight. When I first got married I absolutely *loved* the way I looked. I was in possibly the best shape of my life. I was energetic, and now I felt like nothing more than a giant blob of fat.

It has taken a lot to overcome some of these struggles, and I still battle some every day. Thankfully, I didn't die when I wanted to, and thankfully I believe in a loving God who comes to His children's aid when we need it. I am also grateful that my wife is also a B.E.S.T. practitioner who has been there to build me up and support me, even when I probably didn't deserve it.

But what do you do if you don't have the luxury of a supportive spouse? What do you do when you feel like you're all alone?

My friend, first and foremost, please know that I care about you and want you to succeed. Even if you feel like no one is in your corner, please know that I am rooting for you. Know that if I can have the success that I've had with all the imperfections that I have, so can you! The thing *not* to do is to focus on your imperfections. I'm not saying you shouldn't recognize them and then do something about them. What I'm saying is not to put more energy than necessary into what's wrong with your life. Remember, whatever you focus on expands. Yes, this means I am saying to stop complaining. Complaining about *anything* is a surefire way to *destroy* your results. Remember, whatever you put energy into, you attract more of. If you are a constant or even an occasional complainer, stop it now! This is what journals are for. You are welcome to complain as much as you want to in writing, because writing is actually a way to release and clear out emotion.

Focus on the times of smooth sailing, not the turbulence. Focus on the things that you *do* want and you may find that you end up with a lot more of them. When moments of turbulence come, recognize each for what it is and then look for the reward that's on its way as long as you get through the turbulence.

T. Harv Eker talks about growing yourself to be bigger than your problems. He says that when we are very small-minded people, most problems can seem extremely daunting. On the flip side, when we constantly work on ourselves through daily improvement and champion training, we can actually grow ourselves to the point where we can deal with virtually any problem.

Have you ever had someone you know come to you and start to complain about some huge problem they had, and while they did so you thought, "I don't see the problem here. What's the big deal?" This is because, at that moment, you were bigger than the problem that person was describing. If, for example, you are a level two person and you're faced with a level five problem, that's going to seem like a pretty big problem, but if you're a level ten person faced with a level five problem, that simply isn't a problem anymore.

One way you do this is by conducting a deep personal inventory. If you have a Higher Power, this would be the time to communicate with Him. If you don't, this would be a good time to get one. Get your success journal and something to write with, kneel down in a place where you will not be disturbed, and ask your Higher Power for a list of everything you need to clean up in your life. This list might be quite extensive if you are anything like me. Then go through the list and begin to right all the wrongs that are on there. If you have a religious leader that you go and confess to, you may want to consider making an appointment with him. I'll never forget the incredible healing power that I felt after I did this. I felt like I was on top of the world. I felt clean for the first time in years.

It's OK to take baby steps if you need to as you go through this process. The purpose of this exercise is not to overwhelm you or make you feel like a horrible person for having so many things to clean up. It is quite the opposite, in fact.

When I was working on overcoming a sugar addiction, I set the goal to go just one whole day without sugar, then seven days, and then thirty days. If ever you desire a feeling of total freedom, go without refined sugar for thirty days. I promise you will feel the difference. Just do what it takes to be a little better tomorrow than you are today.

My friend, I know that the pathway to success and, well, life itself, is not easy. If it were easy, it would not be rewarding. The more you sacrifice and put into something, the more rewarding it can be. I don't know about you, but I *love* rewards, especially when they come in the form of seeing other people feel inspired and empowered by what I have been through and have taught them. This is why I would like to offer you a special gift.

I have mentioned the importance of having a personal mentor in order to accelerate your rate of growth. A two-hour personal mentoring session with a Feel Well, Live Well mentor can cost upwards of $10,000, and is well worth the investment. Because of the skill level of our mentors, who are specifically trained to identify the difficulties and roadblocks each individual student is encountering and then create a personalized plan of action, it is not uncommon for our students to double or triple their investment within thirty days of their first one-on-one appointment. I would like to offer you a special chance to have an appointment one-on-one (or one-on-two if you are married; we like to have spouses present to lend support) with one of our mentors. During this appointment, your mentor will ask you what your specific goals are and why you desire to achieve them, read your body language to identify what your specific blocks are, and create a personal plan of action to help you achieve your goals. Again, such an appointment would usually cost over $10,000, but because you took the time to read this book and begin your journey toward the life of your dreams, if you are absolutely committed to changing your life and making a difference in the lives of others, I would like to offer you a personal mentoring appointment at no charge. This can be done either in person or via Skype. Our hope is that, by offering you this gift, you will kick-start your results and then refer others to this book and to our company. Simply contact us using the information on the back cover, let us know that you have read this book, and set up your appointment.

My friend, it is time to stop being broke. It is time to get over what has been holding you down, and it is time to finally, *finally*, live the life you have always dreamed of. Why? Because you deserve it. I believe in you. Now get out there and do it!

Call to Action

I want to personally thank you for purchasing and reading my book. Because you did, I want to offer you a special "thank you" gift worth over $2,500.00. In order to get the absolute most out of this book, I am offering you two tickets to our next three-day Master Creator event, live in Salt Lake City, Utah, information for which can be found at http://feelwelllivewell.com/master-creator/.

Tickets are usually $1,297.00, but if you will commit to being there for the entire three days and playing full-on as if you had paid full price, you and a guest may register for the next class at *no* charge. To claim your free tickets, please send an email to clientservices@ feelwelllivewell.com and let our team know that you have read this book and would like to attend our upcoming Master Creator event.

Please include the following information for each person who will be attending: First and last name, email address, and phone number (including area code) where a company representative may reach you to confirm attendance.

Do you want to take your life to the next level? Join us at our next Master Creator, and let us help you to do so!

Acknowledgments

Special thanks go out to the amazing mentors I have had in my life, including Heather Bailey, Kris Krohn, T. Harv Eker, Tony Robbins, Leslie Householder, Garrett Gunderson, Dr. Roland Phillips, and Dr. M. T. Morter Jr. Without you, your support, and all that you have taught me, none of this would have been possible.

About the Author

Eric Bailey is a professional mentor, trainer, and advanced holistic healthcare practitioner. Over the years, he has closely observed the habits of highly successful people. Implementing what he has learned, he has seen massive growth in his healthcare practice, health, and relationships, especially with his beautiful wife, Heather.

In one year alone, he grew his monthly income more than a hundredfold, going from welfare to wealthy. He now seeks to share his secrets to success, which absolutely anyone can use. Eric is a powerful motivational speaker and has impacted the lives of thousands of people through his audio training CDs, seminars, personal mentoring programs, and healthcare practice in northern Utah.

His greatest desire is to improve the lives of millions of people around the globe by helping them achieve vibrant health, massive wealth, and successful, loving relationships.